BELIEVE IN JOHN'S GOSPEL

THE CONTENT OF BELIEVE IN THE GOSPEL OF JOHN

G. Michael Cocoris

TABLE OF CONTENTS

Preface

Chapter

PREFACE

According to John 3:16, whoever believes in Jesus Christ has eternal life. That is not a rare reference to believing. In his twenty-one-chapter book, the Apostle John uses the verb "believe" one hundred times. In fact, John says that part of the reason he wrote his Gospel was to help his readers believe and obtain life (20:30-31). Since so much depends on believing, it is imperative to determine the meaning of the word *believe* in the book written to get people to believe so they could obtain eternal life. Our eternal destiny depends on it!

In the 1980s, I wrote *Evangelism: A Biblical Approach*, which included a chapter entitled, "What is Faith?" Assuming that people have to know something before they can believe, I wrote, "If faith presupposes knowledge, what does a person need to know? The object of faith in the New Testament is Jesus Christ. If you were to look up all the occurrences of "believe" and "faith" in the New Testament to see what a person must know about Christ, you would discover that a person must believe four things: (1) that Christ is God (John 20:31) and yet (2) a real man (1 John 4:2) ; (3) that He is the one who died for sins (Rom. 3:25) and (4) rose from the dead (Rom. 10:9).

"In the New Testament, those last two facts are called the gospel (1 Cor. 15:3-5). Mark says to preach the gospel and the one who believes it will be saved. Peter says that the Gentiles heard of the gospel and believed (Acts 15:7). Paul says he is not ashamed of the gospel, for it is the power of God to salvation to everyone that believes (Rom. 1:16).

"The object of faith is Jesus Christ, the God-Man, who died and rose. It is not just any 'Christ.' The object of faith must be the Christ who is offered in the gospel, the one revealed in Scripture." In a footnote, I added, "The Scripture warns that some may preach another Jesus (see Matt. 24:4-5; 2 Cor. 11:4)" (*Evangelism: A Biblical Approach*, p. 74).

Recently, it has been brought to my attention that some teach that all that is necessary to obtain eternal life is for people to believe Jesus is the guarantor of eternal life. When I heard that, my first response was, "There is a sense in which that is true." For virtually all of my Christian life, I have preached that the issue in salvation is trusting Jesus *to get you to heaven*. Or, as Paul would say, "Believe on Him *for* everlasting life" (1 Tim. 1:16; italics added). To obtain eternal life, one must believe that Jesus grants it to those who trust Him, for it is biblical. At the same time, I was uncomfortable with any idea that unbelievers do not have to hear about the death and resurrection of Christ.

The issue is the Gospel of John. Some say that, since the Gospel of John is the only book in the Bible written to teach people how to have eternal life, it is the book that must be used to determine what a person must believe to obtain eternal life. Well, what does the Gospel of John teach a person has to believe? That question has driven me to re-examine the Gospel of John in general and, in particular, its content regarding belief. Here are my conclusions.

G. Michael Cocoris.
Santa Monica, California

CHAPTER 1

THE NATURE OF JOHN'S BOOK

In studying the Gospel of John (or any biblical book), the place to begin is with the simple observation that it is a book. Yes, it is *in* a book—the Bible, but the Bible is a *library of books*. The Gospel of John should be studied *as a book*.

That brings up the issue of the nature of a book. What are the various components of a well-written book? Are those elements in the Gospel of John?

The Nature of Well-Written Books

Authors may not follow the neat order laid out here, but the end product of a well-written book has a subject, a narrowed subject, a message that can be summarized in a single sentence, selected material, an arrangement of that material, and a purpose.

Subject Authors begin by choosing a subject. Their subject is a topic about which they have something to say. Let's suppose an author decides to write on the subject of "marriage."

Narrow Subject Because most subjects are so broad, authors are forced to narrow them. Furthermore, just the size of a book forces authors to narrow their subject to book length. That was true in ancient times when "books" were written on scrolls. One scroll could only hold so much material.

Our imaginary author, who decides to write a book on marriage, cannot cover everything in a single manuscript. No one hardback could cover the history of marriage, the various practices of marriage in different countries, etc. You get the idea. So, she decides to limit her book to "the key to marriage."

The Assertion The next step for authors is to decide what they will say about their narrowed subject which is called the assertion. What is our author going to say is the key to marriage?

The Message The combination of a narrowed subject and what is said about that subject in a well-written book can be (should be) stated in a single sentence. A number of different names, such as thesis, theme, proposition, message, etc., have been used for that single sentence.

The problem is that each of those words has several different meanings. For example, the word "message" can mean "a proposition to be maintained or defended in an argument" or "a dissertation." That is a wide range of meanings, from a single sentence to a whole dissertation. Likewise, the word "theme" can mean either "topic," "subject," or "short essay." Again, the range of meaning is wide, including a simple subject and a whole essay. In music, a theme can mean "a series of notes" or the whole song, as in a "theme song."

It does not matter which word is used to define what authors do, as long as it is understood that it is describing a single-sentence summary of the whole work. In school, teachers have students write a short paper. One of the first things the teacher tells the students to do is write a "message," "topic sentence," or "theme sentence" that summarizes what they intend to say.

At any rate, authors who are effective communicators produce works that can be summarized in a single sentence; their works have an overall, all-encompassing, idea. The message sentence of our ambitious author might be: "The key to marriage is sacrificial love."

The Development of the Message After deciding on their message sentence, authors determine how they will *develop* it. The development of a message involves selecting and arranging material.

Part of developing a message is *selecting material* that demonstrates it. Authors have to determine what to include and what to exclude. The material they include may be autobiographical, biographical, ideas, events, etc., or a combination of these. Our author on marriage might select autobiographical material exclusively and/or she might use autobiographical material for one chapter and the result of her research for another, etc.

Once the material has been selected, it has to be arranged. The very nature of written material called literature is an artistic arrangement. One type of arrangement is chronological, but many other possibilities exist. Another simple way to arrange material is: what it is not versus what it is. The book on the key to marriage could be divided into two parts: what the key to marriage is not and what the key to marriage is. Subdivisions of Part I could be the key to "marriage is not an expensive wedding, an enjoyable honeymoon, an endurance contest, etc." Each of these could be a chapter in Part I.

Purpose Authors, of course, have a purpose for writing. Their purpose may be entertainment, education, exhortation, encouragement, etc.

Often, readers have to figure out the subject, message, development of that message sentence, and purpose of an author by asking questions such as, "What is the author talking about (the subject)? What is the author saying about that subject (the message)? How does the author select and arrange material to develop his or her message? Why is the author writing about this (purpose)?" Sometimes, authors answer these questions in the preface or the introduction. A reader may be able to glean some answers from the Table of Contents.

The Gospel of John

In the Gospel of John, the Apostle tells his readers his subject, message, and purpose toward the end of his book. He informs his readers, "And truly Jesus did many other signs in the presence of His disciples, which are not written in this book, but these are written that you may believe that Jesus is the Christ, the Son of God, and that believing you may have life in His name" (20:30-31). The content of the book reveal how John develops his message.

The Subject: As all authors do, John chose a *subject*—Jesus. He says he is talking about Jesus (20:30),but the content about Jesus is overwhelming. John observed, "And there are also many other things that Jesus did, which if they were written one by one, I suppose that even the world itself could not contain the books that would be written" (21:25). John had to narrow his subject.

The Narrow Subject John tells his readers that he narrowed his subject. He wrote, "And truly Jesus did many other signs in the presence of His disciples, which are not written in this book" (20:30). John limits himself to a *narrow subject*. He does not write a biography of Jesus. He does not begin with the birth of Jesus, as do Mathew and Luke. He does not include the great Galilean ministry of Jesus, as is covered in Matthew, Mark, and Luke. Instead, he focuses on events in the ministry of Jesus in Jerusalem.

The Assertion John says the events in the ministry of Jesus prove that He is the Christ, the Son of God.

The Message Therefore, the overall, all inclusive message of the Gospel of John is that the events in the ministry of Jesus demonstrate that He is the Christ, the Son of God. These terms can be (were) misunderstood. So, John will explain what *he* means by them.

The Development of the Message From the content of his book, it is evident that John *develops* his message by *selecting material* from the ministry of Jesus. Traina says, "*Purposive selectivity characterizes the Bible.* In other words, biblical authors had definite purposes, which motivated the writing and they chose their materials and utilized them in such a way as the best accomplish their purposes" (Traina, p. 59, italics his). Tasker says the Gospel of John is "essentially selective" (Tasker, p. 28). Here is a list of the events from the ministry of Jesus that John chose to include in His book. How these events from the ministry of Jesus develop John's message will be discussed later.

John the Baptist (1:19-34)
The First Disciples (1:35-51)
The First Miracle (2:1-11)
The Cleansing of the Temple (2:12-22)
The Jerusalem Crowd and Nicodemus (2:23-3:21)
John the Baptist (3:22-36)
The Woman at the Well (4:1-42)
The Healing of the Nobleman's son (4:43-53)
The Healing of an Infirmed Man (5:1-47)
The Feeding of the 5000/Walking on Water (6:1-71)
The Feast of Tabernacles (7:1-51)
The Women Caught in Adultery (8:1-59)
The Man Born Blind (9:1-41)
The Discourse on the Good Shepard (10:1-21)
The Raising of Lazarus (11:1-53)
The Anointing at Bethany (12:1-11)
The Triumphal Entry (12:12-19)
The Visit of the Greeks (12:20-50)
The Foot Washing and Dismissal of the Betrayer (13:1-30)
The Announcement of Jesus (13:31-14:7)
Questions and Discussion (14:8-31)
Discourse on Relationships (15:1-16:4)
Discourse on the Holy Spirit (16:5-33)
The Lord's Prayer (17:1-26)
The Arrest and Jewish Trials (18:1-11)
The Trial before Pilate (18:12-19:16)
The Crucifixion (19:17-42)
The Post-Resurrection Appearances (20:1-31)

The material John selects is arranged chronologically, from the ministry of John the Baptist to the post-resurrection appearances of Jesus. To that, he adds a prologue and an epilogue.

The chronological material can further be divided into the public and private ministries of Jesus (12:36). Here is a simple overall outline of the book. Other divisions are possible.

Prologue
Public Ministry of Jesus
Private Ministry of Jesus
Epilogue

Purpose John's stated purpose in writing is to get his readers to believe that Jesus is the Christ, the Son of God so that they can have life (20:31). In his commentary on the Gospel of John, Westcott says John is guided in the selection, arrangement, and treatment of his material by his desire to fulfill his purpose (Westcott, p. xlii). Morris says, "John says plainly that he is out to show Jesus as the Christ, the Son of God. And he does this not in order to give his readers some interesting new information but in order that he may bring them to a place of faith and accordingly to new life in Christ's name" (Morris, pp. 39-40). The purpose of John's Gospel will be discussed in more detail later.

Summary: Authors of well-written books select and arrange material to develop their message to accomplish their purpose.

When John wrote the Gospel that bears his name, he assumed

his readers would read all of it. He would be surprised to see that his work has been chopped up into chapters and small verses, which was not done until centuries after he wrote. To completely comprehend what John is saying, the message of the whole book must be considered. To say the same thing another way, the context of the book as a whole must interpret every sentence in any book.

So, to fully understand the Gospel of John, his subject, message, the development of his message, and purpose must be considered.

CHAPTER 2

THE DEVELOPMENT OF JOHN'S MESSAGE

Authors of well-written books select and arrange material to develop their message. The message sentence of the Gospel of John states that Jesus is Christ, the Son of God (20:31). Does the material John selected develop his message sentence? The following brief review of each episode in the fourth Gospel reveals that he did indeed select material that demonstrates that Jesus is the Christ, the Son of God.

By the way, if a student of a book determines the author's message sentence, but the material in the book does not demonstrate that message sentence, the student has not chosen the correct message sentence. A new suggested message sentence must be selected to see if it explains the work as a whole.

The Prologue

The prologue of the Gospel of John (1:1-18) presents Jesus as the Word (1:1), God (1:1), Creator (1:3), life (1:4), light (1:4), a human (1:14), the only begotten of the Father (1:14), that is, a unique Son (1:18), the Son of God (1:14), who reveals the Father (1:18) and it declares Him to be pre-existent (1:15) and calls Him Christ (1:17). In no uncertain terms, John begins his book with a declaration that Jesus is the Christ (1:17), the Son of God (1:14, 18), which means He is God the Son (1:1, 18).

In light of his statement at the end of the book that he is writing to demonstrate Jesus is the Christ, the Son of God, it is significant that John begins with a description of what *he* means by "the Son of God." He means Jesus is God the Son, the Creator of the universe. The climax of the book is at the end when Thomas says to Jesus, "My Lord and my God" (20:28).

Similarly, Luke begins Acts with a detailed description of what he means by the term "tongues" (Acts 2:4-11). From that point on in the book of Acts, he does not bother to define the term "tongues" every time he uses it because he did that at the beginning of the book. Likewise, at the beginning of his Gospel, John clarifies that by "the Son of God;" he means Jesus is God the Son.

John does not describe what he means by "Christ" in the prologue. He does that later in his book (4:25; 10:24; etc.). No doubt, at the beginning of the ministry of Jesus, people did not understand that the Messiah had come to die and be raised from the dead, but there is also no doubt that John intends for his readers to understand that by the time they finish his book.

The Public Ministry of Jesus

John the Baptist (1:19-34) John the Baptist testifies that he is not the Christ (1:20, 1:25). Since he is speaking to Jewish religious leaders, he uses the term "Christ" to refer to the Old Testament

Messiah. John the Baptist testifies that Jesus is the Son of God (1:34), who was before him (1:30), indicating Jesus' pre-existence, and that Jesus is the Lamb of God who takes away the sin of the world (1:29).

Again, it is significant that at the beginning of his book, John selects material that not only identifies Jesus as the Son of God but also as the Lamb of God, who takes away the sin of the world. Granted, at this point in Jesus' ministry, people did not necessarily understand what that meant, but from John's point of view and for his overall purpose, he is further alerting his readers to who Jesus is. The reader would naturally conclude that John is presenting Jesus as the Son of God, who came to die for the sins of the world.

The First Disciples (1:35-51) Andrew announces to Peter that he has found the Messiah (1:41). Philip informs Nathaniel that they have found "Him of whom Moses in the law, and also the prophets, wrote—Jesus of Nazareth, the son of Joseph" (1:45). Nathaniel confesses that Jesus is the Son of God, the King of Israel (1:49).

In this episode, John selects material that presents Jesus as the Messiah. Admittedly, the disciples did not understand that the Messiah had come to die, but John has already included the testimony of John the Baptist to establish that fact, regardless of what the first disciples might have understood. John wants *his* readers to know that Jesus is the Christ, the Son of God (20:31), and by this point in his book, he has made it clear that he means Jesus is the God in the flesh, the Messiah, who has come to die for the sins of the world. This passage also establishes that John is using the word "Christ" as a reference to the Jewish Messiah, the king of Israel. In his commentary on this passage, Morris says John "writes his whole Gospel to make us see that Jesus is the Messiah."

The First Miracle (2:1-11) Jesus changes water into wine, signifying His creative power as God. To not see the deity of Jesus in this sign-miracle is to miss John's point. The reason he includes these sign-miracles is to demonstrate Jesus is the Christ, the Son of God (Remember 20:30-31.) and by "Son of God," John means God the Son (Remember 1:1-18).

The Cleansing of the Temple (2:12-22) Jesus cleanses the Temple, identified as His Father's house (2:16). He is God the Son. When the disciple saw what He did, it reminded them of Psalm 69:9 (2:17), a messianic psalm. When the Jews asked for a sign, Jesus referred them to His resurrection (2:19-21).

It is significant that at this early stage, John selects an incident that indicates Jesus will be raised from the dead. At the time, the disciple did not get it (2:22; 20:9), but John does not want his readers to miss it. So, he includes this story, even though he has to explain that the disciples did not understand it at the time.

Counting the prologue, John has so far written five panels in his Gospel. In these first five sections, he clearly portrays Jesus to his readers as God in the flesh, who has come to die for the sins of the world and be raised from the dead.

The Conversation with Nicodemus (2:23-3:21) Jesus tells Nicodemus that the Son of Man comes from heaven (3:23) and "As Moses lifted up the serpent in the wilderness, even so must the Son of Man be lifted up" (3:14). This episode includes who Jesus is and what Jesus came to do—die for sin.

John the Baptist (3:22-36) John the Baptist testifies that Jesus is the Christ (Messiah) (3:28-29). In his introduction to this passage, Morris says, "The reader of the Gospel now knows what Jesus wants of men. They know that He demands a radical rebirth. They know that He will die for man's salvation" (Morris p. 236).

The Woman at the Well (4:1-42) Jesus reveals He is the Messiah (4:25-26). Notice, John explains to his readers that Messiah means Christ (4:25). When he says at the end of his book that he writes to show that Jesus is the Christ, he has already made explicit in his book that *he* means by the term "Christ" that Jesus is the promised Messiah.

In this story, the Samaritans conclude Jesus is the Christ, the Savior of the world (4:42). The Christ, the Messiah, is now called the Savior. He is not only the King of Israel (1:49); He is the Savior of the world (4:42).

The Healing of the Nobleman's Son (4:43-53) Jesus heals the nobleman's son, the second sign-miracle (4:54), illustrating He is God (4:50; see comments on 2:1-11 above; Remember 20:30-31.).

The Healing of an Infirmed Man (5:1-47) After the third sign-miracle, the healing of an infirmed man (Remember 20:30-31.), Jesus claims He is equal with the Father. He gives life, and judgment is committed to Him (5:21-23). The religious leaders get it. They accuse Him of breaking the Sabbath and claiming to be equal with God (5:10, 16-18)! This is an important contribution to the overall demonstration of John's message. Even His enemies recognize that Jesus claims to be equal to God.

The Feeding of the 5000/Walking on Water (6:1-71) After the fourth and fifth sign-miracles (Remember 20:30-31..), Jesus claims He is sent from heaven and gives life (6:33). Peter tells Jesus, "You have the words of eternal life. Also, we have come to believe and know that You are the Christ, the Son of the living God" (6:68-69).

In a section where the whole issue is that Jesus is equal with God, Peter confesses that Jesus is the Christ, the Son of God, the very words John uses in his purpose statement (20:31). Is not John saying again that by the "expression "the Christ, the Son of God, he means Jesus is God the Son? As the Messiah, God the Son, Jesus is able to give life.

The Feast of Tabernacles (7:1-51) During the Feast of Tabernacles, the issue is whether or not Jesus is the Christ (7:26-27, 31). The term "Christ" is used five times in this section (7:26, 27, 31, 41, 42). There is no question but that this episode is being used as a reference to the Old Testament promise of the Messiah (7:27, 31, 41-42). Note especially John 7:42: "Has not the Scripture said that the Christ comes from the seed of David and from the town of Bethlehem, where David was?" How could there be any question but that the title "Christ" in this passage means the Old Testament promise of the Messiah? Moreover, when this passage records that "many of the people believed in Him" (7:31), it means they believe Jesus is the promised Messiah because they are the ones who ask, "When the Christ comes, will He do more signs than these which this *Man* has done?" (7:31).

By this point in the book, John has clearly established how he is using the expression "the Christ." So when, at the end of the book, he says he writes to show that Jesus is the Christ, he means the promised Messiah of the Old Testament.

The Women Caught in Adultery (8:1-59) After the incident of the women caught in adultery, Jesus says He was the light of the world (8:12). A dialogue follows in which Jesus also claims He knows His origin and destiny (8:14). He judges no man (8:15). He is from above (8:23). He speaks what He hears from His Father (8:26, 29, 38). He is from God (8:42), knows God (8:55), and claims, before Abraham was I AM (8:58), to be God (Plummer, p. 196).

The Man Born Blind (9:1-41) The word "Christ" occurs in this story and is used in the sense of the promised Messiah (9:22). Jesus asks the blind man He healed, the sixth sign-miracle (Remember 20:30-31.), "Do you believe in the Son of God?" (9:35). When the former blind man says, "Who is He, Lord that I may believe in Him?" (9:36), Jesus says to him, "You have both seen Him and it is He who is talking with you."

The Discourse on the Good Shepard (10:1-21) In this discourse, Jesus claims that He is the door by which people are saved (10:9), that He came that people may have life (10:10), that He lays down His life for the sheep (10:15, 17-18), and that He has the power to take His life again (10:18). John again presents Jesus to his readers as the One who came to die and rise again from the dead.

The Feast of Dedication (10:21-42) During the Feast of Dedication, the Jewish leaders insist, "How long do You keep us in doubt? If You are the Christ, tell us plainly" (10:24). Jesus replies that His works demonstrated that "Father is in Me, and I in Him." (10:37-38). Again, "Christ" is used for the Jewish Messiah.

The Raising of Lazarus (11:1-53) Jesus raises Lazarus, the seventh sign-miracle (Remember 20:30-31.). He tells the disciples, "And I am glad for your sakes that I was not there, that you may believe" (11:15; see also 11:42). Jesus claims to be the resurrection and the life (11:25). Martha confesses, "Lord, I believe that You are the Christ, the Son of God, who is come into the world" (11:27). Martha uses the same expression John says is his purpose for writing (20:31). Other than Jesus being able to give life and raise people from the dead, there is nothing in this immediate context to indicate what the term "Christ" means, but from the context of the book, it is reasonable to assume that it is being used the way John has used it thus far.

The Anointing at Bethany (12:1-11). Mary anointed Jesus for His burial (12:7). John again presents the death of Jesus.

The Triumphal Entry (12:12-19) At the Triumphal Entry, the crowd proclaims Jesus the King of the Jews (12:13). Riding the donkey was a symbolic presentation of Jesus as the Messiah because it fulfilled prophecy (12:14-15). The people who saw the resurrection of Lazarus bore witness to that fact (12:17).

The Visit of the Greeks (12:20-50) After the Greeks request to see Him, Jesus speaks of His death (12:24) and says, "If I am lifted up from the earth, I will draw all peoples to Myself" (12:32).

John adds, "This He said, signifying by what death He would die" (12:33).

When "The people answered Him, 'We have heard from the law that the Christ remains forever; and how *can* You say, 'The Son of Man must be lifted up'? Who is this Son of Man?'" (12:34), they are obviously using the title "Christ" to mean the promised Messiah.

Private Ministry of Jesus

The Foot Washing and Dismissal of the Betrayer (13:1-30) At this point in the Gospel of John, Jesus ceases His public ministry (12:36) and commences a private ministry (13:1-17:26). In the Upper Room Discourse, Jesus tells the disciple that one of them will betray Him so that "when it does come to pass, you may believe that I AM *He*" (13:19). The word "He" is not in the Greek text. This is another reference to the "I AM" of the Old Testament. Jesus wants them to believe He is God.

The Announcement of Jesus (13:31-14:7) When Peter asks where Jesus was going, He says, "You believe in God, believe in Me" (14:1). Westcott, who takes this as two imperatives, says the simultaneous injunction of faith in God and in Christ under the same conditions implies the deity of Christ.

Questions and Discussion (14:8-31) Jesus teaches, "I am in the Father, and the Father in Me" (14:10-11). Jesus also tells them of His departure so "that when it does come to pass, you may believe" (14:29). His prediction in advance would strengthen their faith that He is who He says He is (14:29).

Discourse on Relationships (15:1-16:4) During this private time with His disciple, Jesus claims that He is the true vine (15:1), that without Him we can do nothing (15:5), and that He will send the Holy Spirit (15:26). He also says, "these things I have told you, that when the time comes, you may remember that I told you of them" (16:4).

Discourse on the Holy Spirit (16:5-33). Jesus promises to send the Holy Spirit (16:7). He claims that the Holy Spirit comes from the Father (16:27, 30), another indication that He is the Son of God. He is telling them some things beforehand to strengthen their faith (16:30).

The Lord's Prayer (17:1-26). In His prayer, Jesus uses the title "Christ" of Himself (17:3). He also speaks of His pre-existence (17:5) and of God the Father sending Him (17:8). God the Father sent Jesus, the Son of God.

The Arrest and Jewish Trials (18:1-11) During His arrest and Jewish trial, Jesus is said to know all things (18:34), claims to be "I AM" (18:5-6, 8), and fulfills prophecy (18:8-9). The denials of Peter are a fulfillment of the Lord's prediction. Caiaphas says, "It was expedient that one man should die for the people" (18:14). This passage portrays Jesus as the Christ, the Son of God.

The Trial before Pilate (18:12-19:16) During the trial before Pilate, Jesus is again presented as the Messiah. When Pilate asks if He is King of the Jews (18:33), Jesus replies that He is (18:36-37). The soldiers mock Him as King of the Jews (18:2-3). The Jewish leaders accuse Him of claiming to be the Son of God (19:7) and, according to them, what He means by that is worthy of death (19:7). Pilate offers Jesus to the crowd as their king (19:14).

The Crucifixion (19:17-42) John's account of the crucifixion is filled with indications that Jesus is the Christ. The title Pilate puts on the cross says Jesus is King of the Jews (19:19). The soldiers casting lots for the tunic of Jesus fulfilled Scripture (19:24). John records that Jesus "knew all things were now accomplished, that the Scripture might be fulfilled" (19:28). Both the lack of broken bones and the piercing of His side are the fulfillment of Scripture (19:36-37).

The Resurrection (20:1-31) After the resurrection, which is the eighth sign-miracle, Thomas says that he will not believe it until he sees it for himself (20:25). When Thomas sees the resurrected Christ, He confesses Jesus as "My Lord and My God" (20:28).

Epilogue

In the epilogue (21:1-25), Jesus appears to the Disciples, showing again that He was raised from the dead.

Summary: In every episode in his Gospel, John presents Jesus as the Son of God, that is, God the Son, and in many of them, he presents Jesus as the Christ, the promised Messiah of the Old Testament.

Morris says, "John says plainly that he is out to show Jesus as the Christ, the Son of God." He also says, "Not only does John tell us this in set terms, but close examination of his gospel shows that is, in fact, what he has done" (Morris, pp. 39-40).

Tasker notes, "Our evangelist portrays Jesus as performing a Messianic action in 'cleansing' the temple on His first visit to Jerusalem after His ministry had begun. Moreover, long before the events that led to His final rejection by the religious leaders, Jesus is seen to be engaged in bitter controversy with them in the temple precincts about His Messianic claims to 'work' on the Sabbath, involved in the healing of the paralyzed man at Bethesda, and in the gift of sight to a man born blind. It is as Messiah that His disciples accept Him from the first, even though they are not fully aware of the kind of Messiah He is. It is as Messiah that He reveals Himself to the Samaritan woman, however imperfectly she may understand the title when He applies it to Himself. It is as Messiah that He feeds the hungry Galileans, though He escapes from them as soon as they try to enthrone Him as an earthly monarch. And it is as Messiah that He approaches Jerusalem for the last time, though as soon as He is greeted as a warrior-king, He finds an ass and rides into the city as a king of peace. Two of the constantly recurring themes of this Gospel are the nature of the unbelief which led the Jews to refuse to accept Jesus as the Messiah, and the prerequisites and the constituent factors of the faith which led His disciples to acknowledge Him as the One 'of whom Moses in the law, and the prophets, did write'" (Tasker, p. 29).

The Gospel of John not only shows that Jesus is the Christ, the Son of God, but it presents Christ, the Son of God, as God in the flesh, who died for sin and rose from the dead. At first, the people in the book, not even the disciples, do not understand all that is involved in Jesus being the Messiah, the Son of God, but from the beginning of the book, John wants his readers to understand what *he* means by these terms and what *they* should conclude from them. So, he carefully explains these terms.

According to John, Jesus is God in the flesh. The book opens with that declaration. What could be clearer than "the Word was God" (1:1) and "the Word became flesh" (1:14)? John the Baptist testifies to the pre-existence of Jesus (1:15, 30). The seven sign-miracles performed by Jesus demonstrate the supernatural power of a divine being. Jesus claims to be God (5:21-23). There is no question about that; the religious leaders accuse Jesus of making Himself equal with God (5:10, 16-18)! Jesus claims to be the I AM (8:58, 18:5-6, 8), a clear claim of deity. The book's climax is Thomas's confession that Jesus is his Lord and *God* (20:28).

According to John, Jesus died for sin. John the Baptist points to Jesus as the Lamb of God (1:29). By recording John the Baptist's testimony, John the Apostle signals at the beginning of his book that Jesus came to die for the sins of the world. Jesus tells Nicodemus, "As Moses lifted up the serpent in the wilderness, even so must the Son of Man be lifted up" (3:14). Jesus says that He lays down His life for the sheep (10:15, 17-18). Speaking of His death, Jesus says, "Most assuredly, I say to you, unless a grain of wheat falls into the ground and dies, it remains alone; but if it dies, it produces much grain" (12:24). He also says "And I, if I am lifted up from the earth, will draw all *peoples* to Myself" (12:32) and John explains, "This He said, signifying by what death He would die" (12:33). His arrest, trail, and crucifixion are cover in two chapters (18:1-19:42). More space is given to that than any other event or episode in the entire book, meaning the author wishes to make it a major point of his presentation. In fact, Kahler has described the Gospels as "passion narratives with extended introductions" (cited by France, p. 359). While that is an obvious exaggeration, it highlights the fact that the point of the Gospels is the passion of Jesus. In the words of France, "Kahler put the emphasis in the right place" (France, p. 359). In an article on Martin Luther, Cook concludes, "In his (Martin Luther) estimation, Jesus Christ can never be properly understood apart from Good Friday" (Cook, pp. 339-340).

Tasker observes, "An exaggerated emphasis upon the prologue has sometimes led readers of this Gospel to conclude that redemption through the death of Jesus does not occupy the primary place in the theology of this evangelist that it occupies in the theology of Paul. 'But if,' in the words of James Denney, 'we turn from the prologue to the Gospel itself, in which Jesus actually figures and in which His words and deeds are before us, we receive a different impression…. We find that the death of Christ comes to the fore in a great variety of ways as something of peculiar significance for the evangelist. That the Son of God 'was manifested to take away our sins' (I Jn. iii. 5) is very evident in the Gospel. He did this by laying down His life for the sheep (x. 11). At the outset of the narrative, He is marked out as 'the Lamb of God' destined to take upon Himself, and in so doing to take away the sin of the world (i. 29). By being lifted up on a cross, and only by being lifted up on a cross, He has power to draw all men to Himself (xii. 32, 33). By giving His flesh for the life of the world, He offers men and women God's supreme gift, and unless they 'eat' His flesh and accept His gift, they have no life in them (vi. 33-53). By dedicating Himself and offering the sacrifice of Himself, He makes it possible for others to consecrate their lives to God (xvii. 19). The grain of wheat, He teaches, must fall into the ground and die before it can bring forth fruit; and, in keeping with this principle, which is as true in the spiritual realm as it is in the natural, He Himself must die that men 'may have life and have it in abundance' (xii. 24, x. 10). His whole incarnate life is, in fact, meaningless apart from 'the hour' to which it is inevitably moving, and that hour is none other than the hour of His passion (see ii. 4, vii. 7, 8, 30, xii. 23, xvii. I)." (Tasker, pp. 31-32).

According to John, Jesus rose from the dead. Earlier in His ministry, Jesus says, "Destroy this temple, and in three days I will raise it up" (2:19). John explains, "He was speaking of the temple of His body." Therefore, when He had risen from the dead, His disciples remembered that He had said this to them; and they believed the Scripture and the word which Jesus had said" (2:21-22). Jesus also says He had the power to lay down His life and the power to take it again (10:18). His resurrection and subsequence appearances are covered in two chapters (20:1-21:25).

From beginning to end, the Gospel of John presents Jesus as *the Christ, the Son of God* and from the beginning of the book to the end of the book, the deity, death, and resurrection of Jesus are present, indicating that *the Christ is the God/man, who died for sin and 'rose from the dead.* It is inescapable that, *taken as a whole*, the Gospel of John not only presents Jesus as the Christ, the Son of God, but it also leaves no doubt that Christ is God, who came as a man to die and be raised from the dead. How could anyone read this book and not come to the conclusion that John's message is just that?

CHAPTER 3

THE PURPOSE OF JOHN'S GOSPEL

There is a wide variety of explanations for the purpose of the Gospel of John. For a survey of the suggestions, see Morris, pages 35-40, G. Ted Martinez, "The Purpose of John's Gospel: Part One," *Michigan Theological Journal*, Vol. 3:1, Spring 192, pp. 42-54, and Stephen Smalley, "Keeping Up with Recent Studies—XII. St. John's Gospel," *The Expository Times*, 97, 1986, pp. 102-108. Here is a summary of the major views.

To Refute Heresy

One early view is that John wrote to refute heresy. Irenaeus states that John wrote his Gospel to controvert Cerinthus and, before him, the Nicolaitans. Tertullian basically agreed with him (see Alford, vol. I, p. 57). This is Bultmann and Barrett's position.

Plummer, however, points out, "By clearly teaching the main truths of the Gospel," John necessarily refutes error, but "the refutation of error is not his object in writing (Plummer, p. 36). Westcott says John's purpose is not "specifically polemical" (Westcott, p. xli).

To Supplement the Synoptic Gospels

Another early explanation is that the Gospel of John was written to supplement the Synoptic Gospels (Clement of Alexander). Eusebius says that John wrote because his friends urged him to record what the other Gospels had omitted (Godet, vol. I, p. 209).

Again, it is Plummer who observes that John no doubt supplements the other Gospels but does not follow that he wrote to supplement them (Plummer, p. 36). Westcott concurs, explaining that John analyzes faith and unbelief. The natural consequence is that John records what happened in Jerusalem (Westcott, pp. xli-xlii).

To Create Faith

Actually, John states his purpose. He writes, "And truly Jesus did many other signs in the presence of His disciples, which are not written in this book; but these are written that you may believe that Jesus is the Christ, the Son of God and that believing you may have life in His name" (20:30-31). John says his purpose is evangelistic. In the words of Westcott, the "specific purpose" was to "create a particular conviction" in his readers to bring them to life (Westcott, p. xl). Plummer says something similar, namely, that the object is to "create" a belief that Jesus is the Christ and that He is the Son of God (Plummer, p. 35). Tenney echoes their position, stating, "The express purpose of the Gospel is to create belief" (Tenney, p. 50).

Morris says there is no reason for ignoring this "express statement." John plainly says he is out to show that Jesus is the Christ, the Son of God and he does so to bring his readers to a place of faith and new life in Christ's name. Not only does John say that it is his purpose, but a close examination of his gospel shows that this is, in fact, what he has done. Again and again, he presents evidence that Jesus is the Christ. While he does not use the term extensively, the idea is often present even when he does not. "There seems to be no reason why John's statement should be rejected. This is what he said he would do and this, it seems, is what he has done" (Morris, pp. 39-40).

To Edify Believers

Some say John's purpose statement indicates that John wrote to edify believers (Beasley-Murray, pp. 387-388). Beasley-Murray asserts that the majority of recent scholars hold this position (Beasley-Murray, p. lxxviii).

Several arguments are used to support this position. In the Critical Text, "believe" in John 20:31 is in the present tense. The argument is that the present tense means "continue to believe" and, thus, John primarily writes to believers to strengthen their faith (see Morris, p. 40, fn. 99, Martinez, Part Two, pp. 129-133). The word "therefore" in John 20:30 links the verses stating the purpose (Jn. 20:30-31) to the immediate context of John 20:24-29, where "believe" appears five times. Thomas's faith needs strengthening (Martinez, Part Two, pp. 133-134). Moreover, statements throughout the book indicate that it was the disciples' faith that was strengthened, not unbelievers believing for the first time (2:11; 6:69; 11:4, 15, 40-42; 16:30). In addition, it is argued that John 14-17 concerns believers, not unbelievers. Alford says this Gospel presupposes readers who were already Christians. He said it was written to build them up and confirm them in the faith (Alford, vol. I, prolegomena, p. 57).

There are problems with the position that the Gospel's primary purpose is to strengthen believers' faith. In the first place, the present tense of "believe" in the Critical Text of John 20:31 does not prove the Gospel of John was written for believers to *continually* believe. In fact, the chief aspect of Greek tenses is "kind of action;" "*time is but a minor consideration in the Greek tenses*" (Dana and Mantey, p. 177, italics theirs.). As Morris points out, to draw such a conclusion based on the present tense "seems to be reading a good deal into the tense" (Morris, p. 40, fn. 99).

Also, in the Majority Text, the word "believe" in John 20:30 is in the aorist tense. In other words, the vast majority of manuscripts contain the aorist tense, not the present tense. The kind *of action* of the Greek aorist tense is punctiliar (Dana and Mantey, p. 179). It presents the action as attained. It states the *fact* of the action without regard to its *duration* (Dana and Mantey, p. 193). The aorist tense supports the idea of an evangelistic purpose.

Apart from grammatical considerations, it is clear that throughout his Gospel, John is not so much thinking about believers who need a deeper theology as he is about unbelievers who are concerned about eternal life (C. H. Dodd, *The Interpretation of the Fourth Gospel*, p. 9 cited by Morris, p. 40, fn. 100). "This gospel, unlike the others, answers question, 'What must I do be saved?' The others mainly confined themselves to the story of discipleship; the Fourth Gospel speaks in terms not only of following and imitation but of belief and incorporation" (C. F. D. Moule, *The Birth of the New Testament*, p. 94, cited by Morris, p. 40, fn. 101).

Nevertheless, there are indications in the book that the intent is to confirm and strengthen the faith of those who already believe (2:11; 11:4, 11:15, 11:40-42; 13:19; 14:29; 16:4; 16:30). Hence, some conclude that the purpose of the Gospel is "to bring the readers to faith or confirm them in faith" (Bruce, p. 12).

The Solution

To resolve this issue, consider carefully: 1) John's purpose statement in John 20:30-31, 2) an analysis of the book's content, and 3) some statements throughout the book.

First, John writes "And truly Jesus did many other signs in the presence of His disciples, which are not written in this book; but these are written that you may believe that Jesus is the Christ, the Son of God and that believing you may have life in His name" (20:30-31). Even though this verse does not say "eternal" life, in light of all the statements in the book to the effect that believing results in "eternal" life (for example, 3:15, 3:16. 3:18; etc.), it is inescapable that John's purpose, at least, includes the issue of eternal life.

Nevertheless, notice he says these signs were written so that people might believe and have life. John is not necessarily referring to the whole book; he only says the *signs* were written for an evangelistic purpose and the seven signs all appear in the first half of the book (2:1-11; 4:46-54; 5:1-18; 6:5-14, 6:16-21; 9:1-7; 11:1-45).

At the same time, in several places elsewhere in the book, statements are made that indicate the intent of the author is to strengthen the faith of those who already believe (2:11, 11:4, 11:15, 11:40-42; 13:19; 14:29; 16:30). In addition, there are also passages dealing with discipleship (8:30-32; 13:1-17, 13:34-35; 14:12-26; 15:1-16:15; 17:26; 20:19-23; 19:24-29; 21:1-19). It could be argued that even the passages on discipleship are given to demonstrate that Jesus is the Christ. There may be some truth to that. Yet these passages contain material that is beyond a strict evangelistic purpose.

When all the evidence is considered, it seems that John had a major purpose and several minor purposes in writing his Gospel.

Summary: The major purpose of the Gospel of John is evangelistic; the minor purposes are to strengthen the faith of believers and urge them to become disciples.

The major purpose is to create faith. If Jesus is the Christ, the Son of God, believe Him. If you do, you will have eternal life. That is the *primary* purpose of the book. A minor purpose for demonstrating that Jesus is the Christ, the Son of God, is to strengthen the faith of those who already believe. If Jesus is the

Christ, the Son of God, you can be certain that you have eternal life by believing in Him. Another minor purpose is to encourage believers to become disciples. If Jesus is the Christ, the Son of God, abide in Him.

CHAPTER 4

BELIEF IN JOHN'S GOSPEL

John says he writes to persuade people to believe Jesus is the Christ, the Son of God. In the book itself, what is the content of believing? Here is an analysis of the 100 occurrences of "believe" in the Gospel of John to determine the content of believing in each case. The one hundred occurrences are numbered and the word "believe" is in bold type. If the content of believe is Jesus or something about Him, it is also bold type. If the object of believing is something other than Jesus, the object is underlined. The words in parentheses are Greek words, the significance of which will be discussed in the next chapter.

The Prologue

1. John the Baptist came "to bear witness of the Light that all through him might **believe**" (1:7). In the context of the prologue, the Word is God (1:1), who is the Creator (1:3), Life (1:4) and Light (1:4). Therefore, in this context, for John the Baptist to be a witness of the Light is for him to proclaim Jesus as God. The prologue indicates that John the Baptist believed in the pre-existence of Jesus (1:15). So, believing the witness of John the Baptist is to believe that Jesus is the **Son of God** (1:34), that is, God the Son.

2. Those who **believe in (eis) His name** become children of God (1:12). To believe in the name of Jesus is more than just believing His name is Jesus. In the Bible, a person's name represents who the person is. When Jesus met Simon, He changed his name to Peter, signifying that Simon would become a stone (1:42). The psalmist says, "Those who know Your name will put their trust in You" (Ps. 9:10). Obviously, people do not trust God just because they know His name; they trust Him because they know something about Him, which His name represents. Therefore, believing in the name of Jesus is believing in who He is and in the context of the prologue, Jesus is the **Son of God**, yea, God the Son. Later, John speaks of those who do not "believe in the name of the only begotten Son of God" (3:18), indicating that believing in His name is believing He is the Son. This is confirmed by the use of the phrase "in His name" in John 20:31.

The Public Ministry of Jesus

John the Baptist (1:19-34) The word "believe" is not used in this sub-section, but this story clearly presents Jesus as the Son of God (1:34), who came to die for the sins of the world (1:29).

The First Disciples (1:35-51)

3. When Nathaniel confesses that Jesus is the Son of God, the King of Israel, Jesus asks him if he **believes** (1:49-50). Here, believing is that Jesus is **the Son of God, the King of Israel** (1:49), the Messiah.

The First Miracle (2:1-11)

4. As a result of changing water to wine, His disciples **believed in (eis) Him** (2:11). Because John says that he included sign-miracles so that people would "believe Jesus is the Christ, the Son of God" (20:31), it is safe to assume that "believe" in John 2:11 is the belief that Jesus is the **Son of God**, God the Son. As a result of this miracle, the disciples believed (2:11). Apparently, they believed earlier (1:41, 45, 49). This confirmed their faith.

The Cleansing of the Temple (2:12-22)

5. The disciples do not understand the resurrection of Jesus until after the resurrection (2:22, 20:9), but after the resurrection, "They **believed** the Scripture and the Word which Jesus had said" (2:22). The object of their belief is the Scripture, more specifically, the Scriptural prediction of the resurrection of the Messiah.

The Jerusalem Crowd and Nicodemus (2:23-3:21)

6. "Many **believed in (eis) His name** when they saw the signs which He did" (2:23). Most commentators contend these people did not have real faith because their faith was based on miracles and because Jesus did not commit Himself to them (2:24; Calvin, etc.), but John recorded the miracles of Jesus so that people would believe and have eternal life (20:30-31)! Thomas is an illustration of someone who had to see before he would believe; he saw and believed (20:24-29).

Moreover, the expression to believe "in His name" only appears three times in the Gospel of John and in the two other places it occurs, it describes genuine faith (1:12; 3:18). In fact, John 3:18 specifically says, "He who believes in Him is not condemned, but he who does not believe is condemned already because he has not believed in the name of the only begotten Son of God." The reason they are condemned is that they do not believe in the name of the only begotten Son of God! Hence, here, believing in His name means believing He is the **Son of God.**

7. Jesus did not **"commit** Himself**"** to these believers (2:24). The Greek word translated "commit" in verse 24 is the same word that is translated "believe" in verse 23. They trusted Him; He did not trust them. In the Greek text, this is a play on words. Because they believed in His name, they became children of God (1:12), but beyond that, Jesus did not trust them. Some believers are not trustworthy with such things as money (Lk. 16:11-12). Therefore, the Lord does not trust them with greater responsibilities (Lk. 16:11).

8-9. Jesus tells Nicodemus, "If I told you earthly things and you do **not believe**, how will you **believe** if I tell you heavenly things?" (3:12). Nicodemus originally comes to Jesus, saying, "we" (3:2). In verses 11 and 12, "you" is plural indicating that Jesus is not speaking to just Nicodemus but to the group from which he comes. Nicodemus believes in the miracles of Jesus (3:2), but not all the members of the Sanhedrin do (3:11). Thus, Jesus rebukes them by saying, "If I have told you earthly things, that is, things which take place on earth even though they originate in heaven, such as sign-miracles, how will you believe if I tell you of heavenly things, such as things concerning eternal life?" (3:11-12). Believing in heavenly things is believing **Jesus came from heaven, that is, He is the Son of God** (3:13).

10. Jesus informs Nicodemus, "whosoever **believes in (eis) Him** should not perish but have eternal life" (3:15). From the immediate context, it is obvious that the One in whom a person must believe to have eternal life is the **Son of Man, who came from heaven and is now in heaven (3:13) and who would die to save people** (3:14).

11. God's love motivated Him to send His Son to die so that "whoever **believes in (eis) Him,** that is, **the Son**, should not perish but have everlasting life" (3:16).

12-14. "He who **believes in (eis) Him**, that is, **the Son,** is not condemned, "but he who does **not believe** is condemned already because he has **not believed in (eis) the name of the only begotten Son of God**" (3:18). As in John 3:16, belief in Him is belief in the Son of God, who came from heaven and is now in heaven (3:13) and who would die to save people (3:14). The only difference is that John 3:18 is focusing on what happens to those who do not believe. Belief here is belief **in the name of the only begotten Son.**

John the Baptist (3:22-36)

15. "He who **believes in (eis) the Son** has everlasting life; and he who does not believe the Son shall not see life, but the wrath of God abides on him" (3:36). In the Greek text, "believe" only appears once. The phrase "he who does not believe the Son" is "he who disobeys." God commands all to believe. Not to believe is to disobey. The content of belief is that Jesus is the **Son of God.**

The Woman at the Well (4:1-42)

16. Jesus tells her, "Woman, **believe Me,** the hour is coming

when you will neither on this mountain nor in Jerusalem, worship the Father" (4:21). In this verse, the content of "believe" is the truth about worshipping the Father. Nowhere in this passage is the word "believe" used to describe what the woman did, but it leaves no doubt that she does. This passage contains synonyms for faith, such as "ask" (4:10) and "drink" (4:13-14). What is the content of her belief? Jesus tells her, in essence, that she is a sinner (4:16-18) and that He is the Messiah (4:25-26). She gets the message (4:29).

17. "And many of the Samaritans of that city **believed in (eis) Him** because of the word of the woman who testified, "He told me all that I ever did" (4:39). The *reason* she believed was that Jesus told her all she had done, but the *content* of her belief was she was a sinner (4:16-18) and He was the Messiah (4:25-26, 29). So the Samaritans believed He was the **Messiah** (4:42).

18. As a result of Jesus staying in the city of Samaria, "many more **believed** because of His own word" (4:41). The next verse indicates that what they believed was that Jesus is the **Christ, the Savior of the world**.

19. "Then they said to the woman, 'Now **we believe**, not because of what you said, for we have heard for ourselves and know that this is indeed the **Christ, the Savior of the world**'" (4:42). They believed that Jesus was the Messiah and what they meant by that was that He was the Savior of the world.

The Healing of the Nobleman's Son (4:43-53)

20. Jesus says, "Unless you people see signs and wonders, you will by no means **believe**" (4:48). The content of belief is not stated, but, in the context of the Gospel of John, there is no doubt

this is belief that **Jesus is the Christ, the Son of God**, because John plainly says he records sign-miracles so that people would believe Jesus is the Christ, the Son of God (20:30-31).

21. When Jesus tells the Nobleman, "Go your way; your son lives" (4:50), "the man **believed** <u>the word that Jesus spoke</u> to him" (4:50). The man believed the promise of Jesus that his son would be healed.

22. After the man learned the exact time his son was healed, **"he himself believed,** and his whole household" (4:53). Again, the content of the belief is not stated, but the next verse points out that this was the second sign Jesus did in Galilee and John's purpose in recording the sign-miracles is so that people will believe Jesus is the Christ, the Son of God (20:30-31). So, the content of the belief in this verse is that **Jesus is the Christ, the Son of God** (Westcott). Hodges explains it this way: "Your son lives! There was life in that utterance and the nobleman could not now resist the next conclusion. A person who could speak these words with such a result, unhindered by the hills and the valleys which separated him from the one about whom he spoke them, must be more than a mortal man. After all, had it not been the *word* of the Creator/God that had created all things to leap from nothingness into being" (Zane C. Hodges, *The Hungry Inherit*, p. 41).

23. Jesus says, "Most assuredly, I say to you, he who hears My word and **believes in (tw) Him who sent Me** has everlasting life, and shall not come into judgment, but has passed from death into life" (5:24). This time, Jesus gives two requirements for eternal

life: hearing and believing. To have eternal life, people must hear, that is, understand, something. In this context, the something is that Jesus is equal to God. Instead of saying, "Believe in Jesus for eternal life," Jesus says, "Believe in the One who sent Him." **To believe in the One who sent Him is to believe in the Son**. Believing or not believing in God is believing or not believing in what God said about His Son. In his first epistle, John writes, "He who believes in the Son of God has the witness in himself; he who does not believe God has made Him a liar because he has not believed the testimony that God has given of His Son" (1 Jn. 5:10).

24. Jesus says, "And the Father Himself, who sent Me, has testified of Me. You have neither heard His voice at any time nor seen His form. But you do not have His word abiding in you, because **whom He sent, Him you do not believe**. You search the Scriptures, for in them you think you have eternal life; and these are they which testify of Me" (5:37-39). The Father has born witness of Jesus through the Old Testament Scriptures, but the Jewish leaders do not **believe Jesus** because they do not understand what God *the Father* says in the Scripture about *the Son*. When Paul defines the gospel by which we are saved, he says Jesus died for our sins and rose from the dead *according to the Scripture* (1 Cor. 15:1-4).

25. Jesus tells them, "How can you **believe**, who receive honor from one another and do not seek the honor that comes from the only God?" (5:44). The content of their faith is believing what Jesus is telling them about being **equal with God**.

26-29. Jesus also says, "But if you **believed** <u>Moses</u>, you would **believe Me**; for he wrote about Me" (4:46). "But if you do not **believe** <u>his writings</u>, how will you **believe My words**?" (5:47). The content of belief in these two verses is believing Moses (twice) and believing Jesus (twice). Believing is believing what Moses said about **the Messiah** and believing Jesus is believing what He says about being **equal with God.**

The Feeding of the 5000/Walking on Water (6:1-71) After feeding of the 5000 and walking on water, Jesus tells the crowd that followed Him they sought Him because He feed them and that they should *labor* for the food that endures to eternal life (6:17). Jesus quickly clarifies that He is the One who *gives* eternal life (6:18). Eternal life is a gift (4:10; Rom. 3:23). In other words, laboring for eternal life is a synonym for faith. Nevertheless, they did not get the difference between work and give, so they said to Him, "What shall we do, that we may work the works of God?" (6:28).

30. Jesus replies, "This is the work of God, that you **believe in (eis) Him whom He sent** (6:29). The content of believing is that **Jesus is sent from heaven and gives life** (6:33).

31. They request a sign "that we may see it and **believe** You? (6:30). They wanted to see a sign before they believed what He was saying about **being equal with God.**

32. Jesus tells them, "I am the bread of life. He who comes to Me shall never hunger, and he who **believes in (eis) Me** shall never thirst" (6:35). The content of belief is Jesus, who is **the bread of life.**

33. Jesus adds that they have seen Him, but they **do not believe** (6:36). They did not believe that Jesus is **the bread of life**.

34. Jesus says, "And this is the will of Him who sent Me, that **everyone who sees the Son and believes in (eis) Him** may have everlasting life; and I will raise him up at the last day" (6:40). The two conditions for eternal life are to see and to believe. The Greek word translated "sees" means "to look at, gaze, perceive, discern." It is a strong word that is better translated as "contemplates" (Plummer). They had to discern something about Him before they believed in Him. They see Him, but they do not contemplate Him to believe, receive eternal life, and be resurrected later. The content of believe is seeing **the Son**.

35. The Jewish leaders object that Jesus says He came down from heaven (6:41-42). Instead of discussing how He came into the world, for example, the incarnation, He explains the way by which *they may come to Him*. "No one can come to Me unless the Father who sent Me draws him; and I will raise him up at the last day" (6:44). To "come to me" is synonymous with believing in Him. Jesus goes on to say, "Not that anyone has seen the Father, except He who is from God; He has seen the Father. Most assuredly, I say to you, he who **believes in (eis) Me** has everlasting life" (6:46-7). The object of believing is Jesus, the One who has seen the *Father*, which means He is **the Son**.

Jesus goes on to say that He is the bread of life (6:48), which comes down from heaven, and the one who eats it will not die (6:50). He adds, "If anyone eats of this bread, he will live forever; and the bread that I shall give is My flesh, which I shall give for the life of the world" (6:51). Eating the bread, which is His flesh, is a synonym for faith, as is drinking His blood (6:53-54; *cf.* "Whoever eats My flesh and drinks My blood has eternal life" in 6:54; see also 6:58). In this passage, "abide" is also a synonym for faith (6:56). "

36-37. Jesus tells His "disciples" (6:60) that "some of you **do not believe**" (6:64). John adds, "For Jesus knew from the beginning who they were who **did not believe**, and who would betray Him" (6:64b). The content of what they did not believe is not given, but they are in contrast o the disciples who believed that **Jesus is the Christ, the Son of the living God**.

38. Peter says, "Lord, to whom shall we go? You have the words of eternal life. Also, we have come **to believe** and know that You are the Christ, the Son of the living God" (6:68-69). The similarity between the confession of Peter and the purpose statement of John is inescapable (20:30). The content of Peter's faith is that Jesus is the **Messiah, the Son of God**.

The Feast of Tabernacles (7:1-51)

39. In the introduction to this story, John says, "His brothers **did not believe in (eis) Him**" (7:5). They did not believe He was the **Messiah**.

40. "Many of the people **believed in (eis) Him**, and said, "When the Christ comes, will He do more signs than these which this *Man* has done?" (7:31). Clearly, the content of the belief of these citizens of Jerusalem is that Jesus is the **Messiah**. That is the issue in this passage (7:26-27)!

41. Jesus says, "He who **believes in (eis) Me**, as the Scripture

has said, out of his heart will flow rivers of living water" (7:38). The content of believing on Him is not stated in this verse but earlier in this same episode, some of the residents of Jerusalem believed on Him (7:31) and the content of their belief was that Jesus was the **Messiah.**

42. Jesus explained that "He spoke concerning the Spirit, whom those **believing in (eis) Him** would receive" (7:39). Again, the content of their belief is not stated in this verse, but the context indicates it is that Jesus is the **Messiah**.

43. The Pharisees ask, "Have any of the rulers or the Pharisees **believed in (eis) Him**?" (7:48). Again, the content of their belief is not stated in this verse, but the context indicates that it was that Jesus is the **Messiah**.

The Women Caught in Adultery (8:1-59)

44. During that discussion, after the incident of the women caught in adultery, Jesus tells them that if they did not **"believe that (oti) I am He,"** they would die in their sins (8:24). The word "He" is not in the Greek text; it just reads "I AM." Every Jew immediately understood the term "I am" as a claim to be **God** (Plummer). In other words, Jesus is not saying they did not believe that He was the Messiah, but that He was not Jehovah (cf. 8:58).

45. Later, some in the crowd did **"believe in (eis) Him"** (8:30). Although the content of their belief is not stated, it is evident from the context of the conversation that what they believed was that Jesus was **God**.

46. Jesus tells those who **"believed Him"** (8:31) that if they continued in His word, they would be His disciples indeed. These

are the same people of whom it is said that they believed in Him in the previous verse. Therefore, the content of their belief is that He is **God**.

47. Jesus tells the unbelieving Jews, "I tell the truth, you do not **believe Me**" (8:45). They did not believe He was **God**.

48. Jesus says again, "If I tell the truth, why do you not **believe Me**? (8:46). Again, they did not believe He was **God**.

49. As a result of healing a man who was blind from birth, Jesus got into another dialogue. Some of the Pharisees did not **believe** that the man had been healed (9:18).

50. Jesus asked, "Do you **believe in (eis) the Son of God**?" (9:35). Obviously, the content of believing here is that **Jesus is the Son of God**.

51. The former blind man said, "Who is He, Lord that I may **believe in (eis) Him**?" (9:36). The content of the belief is that Jesus is the **Son of God** (9:35).

52. When Jesus said to him, "You have both seen Him and it is He who is talking with you," the healed man said, "Lord, **I believe**!" (9:38). He believed that Jesus was the **Son of God**.

The Discourse on the Good Shepard (10:1-21) The discourse on the Good Shepherd in chapter 10 is the conclusion of the dialogue that began in chapter 9 (*cf.* 9:40 with "you" in 10:2). The word "believe" does not make an appearance in this discourse, but this passage presents Jesus as the Good Shepard, who will die and be raised from the dead.

The Feast of Dedication (10:21-42) At the Feast of Dedication, the Jewish leaders insist, "How long do You keep us in doubt? If

You are the Christ, tell us plainly" (10:24).

53. Jesus tells the Jewish leaders that **they do not believe** (10:25). Since this is in answer to their question as to whether or not He is the Messiah (10:24), obviously, the content of belief here is that Jesus is the **Messiah**.

54. Again, Jesus tells them that they **do not believe** (10:26). This time, He adds that their unbelief stems from the fact that they are not of His sheep (10:26), but, again, they do not believe that Jesus is the **Messiah**.

55-58. Jesus says, "If I do not do the works of My Father, **do not believe Me**; but if I do, though you do **not believe Me**, **believe the works**, that you may know and **believe that (oti) the Father is in Me, and I in Him**" (10:37-38). Jesus says that if He does not do the works of God the Father, they should not believe what He says about Himself, namely, that He is the Messiah (10:24). On the other hand, if He does do the works of the Father, they should believe the works that they may know that He is **God**.

59. At this point, Jesus journeys to Perea, where, according to the testimony of John the Baptist (10:41), many **believe in (eis) Him** (10:42). John testified concerning the **deity of Jesus** (1:26-27, 30, 34) and the **death of Jesus** (1:29).

The Raising of Lazarus (11:1-53)

60. Jesus tells the disciples that He was glad He was not present when Lazarus was sick before He died so that He could raise Lazarus from the dead and they "**may believe**" (11:15). The disciples had already believed (2:11, 7:69), but each new trial offers an opportunity for the growth of their faith that Jesus is the

Christ, the Son of God.

61-62. Jesus tells Martha, "I am the resurrection and the life. He who **believes in (eis) Me**, though he may die, he shall live. And whoever lives and **believes in (eis) Me** shall never die" (11:25-26). Because John wrote that people might believe that Jesus is the Christ, the Son of God (20:31) and Martha uses those very words in her confession in the next verse, believing in Him in this verse is believing that He is **the Christ, the Son of God.**

63. He pointedly asks Martha, "Do you **believe this**?" (11:26). In this case, there is no doubt that the content of believe is that **Jesus is the resurrection and the life and that believing in Him gives eternal life.**

64. Martha replies, "Yes, Lord, **I believe that (oti) You are the Christ, the Son of God, who is come into the world**'" (11:27). Instead of saying that she believes that Jesus is the resurrection and the life, Martha says she believes that **Jesus is the Christ, the Son of God.** Does that not indicate that she is saying her belief in Jesus being the Messiah, the Son of God, includes that He is able to give life and resurrection from the dead to those who believe *in* Him? Note "believe that" (oti) in this passage includes "believe in" (eis).

65. Later, Jesus says to Martha, "Did I not say to you that **if you would believe** you would see the glory of God?" (11:40). Nowhere in this passage is it recorded that Jesus told Martha she would see the glory of God. This apparently refers to His statement that **He is the resurrection and the life** (11:25-26). Perhaps earlier, Jesus said more to her than is recorded.

66. In His prayer, Jesus says, "Father, I thank You that You have heard Me. And I know that You always hear Me, but because of the people who are standing by I said this, that they may **believe that (oti) You sent Me**" (11:42). The content of the belief here is that **Jesus is sent from God.**

67. John records that many of the Jews, who had seen the things Jesus did, "**believed in (eis) Him**" (11:45). They at least believed that Jesus could raise people from the dead and they concluded, as did Martha, that He was the **Messiah.**

68. The chief priests and the Pharisees say, "If we let Him alone like this, **everyone will believe in (eis) Him** and the Romans will come and take away both our place and nation" (11:48). The chief priests and the Pharisees were fearful that the people would believe that Jesus was the **Messiah.**

The Anointing at Bethany (12:1-11) At a dinner in Bethany, Mary anointed Jesus. He says it is for His burial (12:7).

69. Because of Lazarus, many **believed in (eis) Jesus** (12:11). They at least believed that He could raise people from the dead (12:13, 12:17) and probably believed that He is the **Messiah** (11:27, 12:13).

The Triumphal Entry (12:12-19) The word "believe" does not appear in John's account of the Triumphal Entry of Jesus into Jerusalem, but the crowd proclaims Jesus the King of the Jesus (12:13). Riding the donkey was a symbolic presentation of Jesus as the Messiah because it fulfilled prophecy (12:14-15). The people who saw the resurrection of Lazarus bore witness to that fact (12:17).

The Visit of the Greeks (12:20-50) After the Greeks requested to see Jesus, Jesus delivered a discourse, which was interpreted by a voice from heaven and an editorial comment from John.

70. When Jesus spoke of His death (12:24, 32-33) and the people did not understand (12:34), He told them, "While you have the light, **believe in the (eis) light**, that you may become sons of light" (12:36). The content of belief is belief in the light. Jesus, of course, is the light. In this context, He is **the Messiah** (12:34), **the One who is about to die** (12:23-24, 32-33).

71. John reports, "But although He had done so many signs before them, **they did not believe in (eis) Him**" (12:37). They did not believe that Jesus was the Messiah (12:34), because they interpreted the Old Testament to mean that **the Messiah would remain forever and Jesus just said He was going to die** (12:34).

72. John explains their unbelief by quoting Isaiah 53:1, which says, "Lord, who has **believed** <u>our report</u>? And to whom has the arm of the Lord been revealed?" (12:38). By quoting Isaiah, John is saying that the Scriptures themselves teach that **not all will believe in the Messiah** (12:34).

73-74. John says, "Therefore **they could not believe**" (12:39) and he quotes Isaiah 6:10, which says, "He has blinded their eyes and hardened their heart, lest they should see with their eyes and understand with their heart, lest they should turn so that I should heal them." They could not believe Jesus is the **Messiah** (12:34) because of their spiritual blindness. John goes on to say, "Nevertheless, even among the rulers many **believed in (eis) Him**" (12:42). Many of the religious leaders did believe Jesus is the **Messiah** (12:34).

75-76. Jesus says, "He who **believes in (eis) Me, believes not in (eis) Me but in Him who sent Me**" (12:44). In this context, to believe in Jesus is to believe that He is the **Messiah** (12:34). Jesus Christ was the personal manifestation of God. To see Him was to see God. To reject Him was to reject God.

77. Jesus also says, "**Whoever believes in (eis) Me** should not abide in darkness" (12:46). To believe in Jesus is to believe that He is the **Messiah** (12:34). As was indicated earlier in the Gospel of John, Jesus, as the light of the world, reveals God (chapter 1), exposes sin (chapter 8) and reveals the purpose of existence (chapter 9). Anyone who believes in Jesus knows God and should not remain in sin or purposelessness.

78. Jesus says, "And if anyone hears My words and **does not believe**, I do not judge him; for I did not come to judge the world but to save the world (12:47). To not believe is not to believe Jesus is the **Messiah** (12:34). The purpose of Jesus' coming was not to judge, but to save. Jesus goes on to explain, "He who rejects Me, and does not receive My words, has that which judges him—the word that I have spoken will judge him in the last day" (12:48). The one who rejects Him will have the words of Jesus judge him at the judgment.

PRIVATE MINISTRY OF JESUS

The Foot Washing and Dismissal of the Betrayer (13:1-30)

79. After revealing that one of them would betray Him, he

says, "Now I tell you before it comes that when it does come to pass, **you may believe that (oti) I am He**" (13:19). The word "He" in verse 19 is not in the Greek text. Jesus wants them to believe that He is **God**!

The Announcement of Jesus (13:31-14:7)

80-81. When Peter asks where Jesus is going, He says, "**You believe in God, believe in (eis) Me**" (14:1). Westcott, who takes this as two imperatives, says that the simultaneous injunction to believe in God and in Christ under the same conditions implies the **deity of Christ**.

Questions and Discussion (14:8-31) As a result of the Disciples asking questions, there is a discussion.

82. In answer to a question asked by Philip, Jesus says, "**Do you not believe that (oti) I am in the Father, and the Father in Me**? (14:10). The content of believe (in the singular) in this verse is the **union of the Father and Son. Jesus is God in the flesh, the Son of God.**

83-84. Jesus goes on to say, "**Believe Me that (oti) I am in the Father and the Father in Me,** or else **believe Me** for the sake of the works themselves" (14:11). Again the content of believe (in the plural) is the **union of the Father and Son** and they are invited to believe Jesus because of the works He has done.

85. Jesus adds, "He who **believes in (eis) Me**, the works that I do he will also do; and greater works than these he will do because I go to My Father" (14:12). The content of believe is to believe in Jesus, who is the **Son in union with the Father**. Believers will do works greater in extent than Jesus, who worked only in

Palestine.

86. Jesus announces His departure so "that when it does come to pass, you may believe" (14:29). His prediction in advance would strengthen their faith that He is who He says He is. In this context, the issue is **the union of the Father and the Son.**

Discourse on Relationships (15:1-16:4) In this discourse, Jesus claims that He is the true vine (15:1), that without Him, we can do nothing (15:5), and that He will send the Holy Spirit (15:26). The word "believe" does not appear in this discourse, but He tells them that they will be hated of the world (15:18-19) and the world will kill them thinking they are doing God a service (16:2). He says, "But these things I have told you, that when the time comes, you may remember that I told you of them" (16:4). Again, He is telling them something ahead of time to strengthen their faith.

Discourse on the Holy Spirit (16:5-33)

87. Jesus says the Holy Spirit will convict the world "of sin **because they do not believe in (eis) Me**" (16:9). The content of believe is not spelled out, but in the context of the Gospel of John, it is safe to assume that Jesus is saying the world does not believe He is the **Christ, the Son of God**.

88. Jesus says, "For the Father Himself loves you, because you have loved Me, and have **believed that (oti) I came forth from God**" (16:27). Here, it is clear that the content of belief is that **Jesus came from the Father**. Because they recognized Jesus as the Son sent by the Father, not merely as a prophet sent by God, they won the Father's love.

89. The disciples tell Jesus, "See, now You are speaking plainly, and using no figure of speech! Now we are sure that You know all things and have no need that anyone should question You. By this, we **believe that (oti) You came forth from God**" (16:30). His supernatural knowledge proved His divine mission. They believed **He was from God**.

90. Jesus asked, "Do you now **believe**? (16:31). In this context, Jesus is asking if they believe **He is from the Father, that is, is He the Son of God**.

The Lord's Prayer (17:1-26) In His prayer, Jesus speaks of His pre-existence (17:5).

91. In His prayer, Jesus says, "For I have given to them the words which You have given Me; and they have received them, and have known surely that I came forth from You; and they have **believed that (oti) You sent Me**" (17:8). The disciple believed that **God the Father sent Jesus. Jesus is the Son of God**.

92-93. Jesus also says, "I do not pray for these alone, but also for those who will **believe in (eis) Me** through their word; that they all may be one, as You, Father, are in Me, and I in You; that they also may be one in Us, that the **world may believe that (oti) You sent Me**" (17:20-21). Jesus prayed for those who would believe in Him through the testimony of the Apostles. The content of their belief is that **God the Father sent Jesus. Jesus is the Son of God** (17:8). He also prayed that, through the testimony of these converts, the world would believe that **God the Father sent Jesus.**

The Arrest and Trials (18:1-11) This passage records the arrest and trials of Jesus before Annas and Caiaphas, as well as Peter's denials. The word "believe" does not appear here, but Jesus is said to know all things (18:34), claims to be "I AM" (18:5-6, 8), and fulfills prophecy (18:8-9). The denials of Peter are a fulfillment of the Lord's prediction. Caiaphas says, "It was expedient that one man should die for the people" (18:14). This passage portrays Jesus as the Christ, the Son of God.

The Trial before Pilate (18:12-19:16) Like the episode before, this part of the story does not contain the word "believe," but Jesus is again presented as the Messiah. When Pilate asks if He is King of the Jews (18:33), Jesus replies that He is (18:36-37). The soldiers mock Him as King of the Jews (18:2-3). The Jewish leaders accuse Him of claiming to be the Son of God (19:7) and, according to them, what He means by that is worthy of death (19:7). Pilate offers Jesus to the crowd as their king (19:14).

The Crucifixion (19:17-42) John's account of the crucifixion is filled with indications that Jesus is the Christ. The title Pilate put on the cross said Jesus is the king of the Jews (19:19). The soldiers casting lots for the tunic of Jesus fulfilled Scripture (19:24). John records that Jesus "knew all things were now accomplished, that the Scripture might be fulfilled" (19:28). Both the lack of broken bones and the piercing of His side were the fulfillment of Scripture (19:36-37). John does not mention it, but this burial fulfills prophecy (Isa. 53:9).

94. John says he gives this eyewitness account so that his readers may **believe** (19:35). This statement's immediate context can only mean believing that Jesus is **the Christ.**

The Resurrection (20:1-31) John records events surrounding the resurrection.

95. After the resurrection, Peter visits the empty tomb. John says that Peter, "went in also; and he saw and **believed**" (20:8). Peter believed that **Jesus had been raised from the dead.**

96. Thomas says, "Unless I see in His hands the print of the nails, and put my finger into the print of the nails, and put my hand into His side, **I will not believe**" (20:25). At this point, Thomas refuses to believe that **Jesus was raised from the dead.**

97-98. Jesus tells Thomas, "Thomas, because you have seen Me, you have **believed**. Blessed are those who have not seen and **yet have believed**" (20:29). In both cases, the content of the word "believe" here is belief in the **resurrection.**

99-100. John writes, "And truly Jesus did many other signs in the presence of His disciples, which are not written in this book, but these are written that you may **believe that (oti) Jesus is the Christ, the Son of God**, and that **believing** you may have life in His name" (20:30-31). Based on John's own statement as to why he records sign miracles, the only possible conclusion is that he intended all of them to persuade the reader that **Jesus is the Christ, the Son of God.** Moreover, by **believing in His name** they would have eternal life.

Not all the occurrences of the word "believe" in the Gospel of John pertain to Jesus. Jesus does not commit Himself to those who believe in Him (2:24). The Nobleman believes his son is healed (4:50). The Pharisees do not believe the blind man is healed (9:18). There are other examples [see 2:22; 4:21; 5:47 (twice); 12:3].

Of the ninety-two times the word "believed" concerning Jesus, the content of believing is Jesus is the Son of God (1:49; etc.), the Christ (4:42; etc.), the King of the Jews (1:49), come down from heaven (3:15), the Savior of the world (4:42), is equal with God (5:44, 5:47, 6:30), gives life (6:29), is the Bread of life (6:35, 6:36), is God ("I AM" in 8:24; 13:19), sent into the world by God the Father (11:42; 17:8, 17:21) is in the Father and the Father is in Him (10:37, 10:38; 14:10, 14:11, 14:12, 14:29), is the Light (12:36), came to die (3:15; 10:42; 12:36, 12:37) and was resurrected (20:8, 20:25. 20:29).

Summary: The content of believing in Jesus in the Gospel of John is believing Jesus is the Christ, the Son of God, that is, God the Son, who was sent into the world by God the Father to be the Savior of the world and to give life by dying for the sins of the world and being raised from the dead.

The Gospel of John states that Jesus was a man (1:14), but it does not make an issue of believing that He came in the flesh. However, when John wrote his first epistle, it was an issue. Hence, he emphatically declares that not to confess that Jesus has come in the flesh is to demonstrate that you are not of God (1 Jn. 4:1-3). In the Gospel of John, believing that Jesus came in the flesh is assumed, but when some denied it, the obvious is stated plainly. Likewise, taken as a whole, the Gospel of John assumes the reader gets the message that Jesus, God the Son, who became a man, died for sin and rose from the dead. It is that individual who must be trusted for eternal life.

The objection to such a conclusion is that people in the book, of whom it is said that they believed, did not understand that the Messiah was going to die and be raised from the dead. It is true that *before* the cross and resurrection, people did not necessarily understand that the Messiah would die and be raised from the dead. John even says that before the resurrection, the Disciples did not believe the Messiah "must rise again from the dead" (20:9). Nevertheless, several things must be considered.

In the first place, before the crucifixion and resurrection, the people may not have understood it, but in some cases, the message of the Messiah's death and resurrection is *presented* to them. John the Baptist announces that Jesus is the Lamb of God, who takes away the sin of the world (1:29). Jesus tells the people in Jerusalem about His resurrection (2:19-22). Jesus tells Nicodemus about the cross (3:15), etc.

In the second place, John writes that, from the beginning, after the death and resurrection of Jesus, he proclaims Jesus as Christ, the Son of God, who would die and be raised. Regardless of what those *before* the cross did or did not understand, there is no doubt that John intends his readers, after the resurrection of Jesus, to understand that Jesus is the Christ, the Son of God, who was sent from God to die and be raised from the dead. Statements throughout the book and in its last chapters demand such a conclusion. It is immediately after Jesus demonstrates His resurrection to Thomas that John says that what He writes is so people may believe that Jesus is the Christ, the Son of God (20:31). Did he not intend that part of believing that Jesus is the Christ, the Son of God is believing that He is the One who died and rose from the dead? Besides, how could anyone read the entire Gospel of John and not understand what John intends for his readers to know about the deity, death, and resurrection of Jesus, the Christ? A third of John's Gospel is used to record the last week in the life and ministry of Jesus.

In the third place, what *Jesus commands* and what the *apostles do and say* confirm that we are to preach the gospel, which is defined as Jesus dying for our sins and rising from the dead. Granted, before the cross, not all understood that Christ would die and be raised from the dead (Mt. 16:16-23; Jn. 20:9), but what happens *before* the cross is not necessarily the norm *after* the cross. It is simply undeniable that after the cross, the norm is for us to preach the gospel, defined as the death and resurrection of Jesus Christ.

After He died and before He ascended, Jesus commissioned the Apostles to preach the gospel (Mk. 16:15). The Greek word translated "gospel" simply means "good news." In the New Testament, it does not necessarily mean the good news about Jesus Christ (1 Thess. 3:6), but in the context of the latter part of Mark, the word "gospel" is used to include Christ's death (Mk. 14:3-9, esp. "this gospel" in Mk. 14:9).

Furthermore, in the context of the post-resurrection ministry of Jesus, during which time He gave the Apostles the Great Commission, He made it clear that from that point, they were to preach His death and resurrection. He says, "Thus it is written, and thus it was necessary for the Christ to suffer and to rise from the dead the third day and that repentance and remission of sins should be preached in His name to all nations, beginning at Jerusalem" (Lk. 24:46-47). Notice that Jesus says the Christ must suffer and be raised from the dead. Did John not know that, after the resurrection, Jesus taught that this is the way Christ is to be presented? Did he not do that very thing in his Gospel—from beginning to end?

Peter finally gets the point. In Acts, he preaches the death and resurrection of Jesus, proclaiming that the death and resurrection of Jesus prove He is the Christ! (Acts 2:22-36, esp. 2:36; 3:12-26, esp. 3:18; and 3:26; 4:9; 5:29-32; 10:36-43). He told the Jerusalem council, "God chose among us, that by my mouth the Gentiles should hear the word of the gospel and believe" (Acts 15:7).

Paul does the same thing. Luke says, "Then Paul, as his custom was, went in to them, and for three Sabbaths reasoned with them from the Scriptures, explaining and demonstrating that the Christ had to suffer and rise again from the dead, and *saying,* 'This Jesus whom I preach to you is the Christ'" (Acts 17:2-3). Notice it is Paul's *custom* to preach the gospel, that is, the death and resurrection of Christ.

Paul says to the Corinthians, "It pleased God through the foolishness of the message preached to save those who believe" (1 Cor. 1:21) and he goes on to identify the message when He writes, "We preach Christ crucified" (1 Cor. 1:23). Paul reminds the Corinthians that they were saved by believing the gospel, that is, the good news that Jesus died for their sins and 'roes from the death (1 Cor. 15:1-5). Notice Paul specifically says they were saved by *believing the gospel* (1 Cor. 15:2), which he defines as the death and resurrection of Christ (1 Cor. 15:3-5). To get *saved*, they *believed that Jesus died for their sins and rose from the dead.*

Paul writes to the Galatians, "O foolish Galatians! Who has bewitched you that you should not obey the truth, before whose eyes Jesus Christ was clearly portrayed among you as crucified?" (Gal. 3:1). In other words, Paul preaches Christ crucified to the Galatians when he evangelized them.

Paul reminds the Thessalonians that "our gospel did not come to you in word only, but also in power, and in the Holy Spirit and in much assurance" (1 Thess. 1:5). He preaches the gospel, the death and resurrection of Christ (1 Cor. 15:1-5), to the Thessalonians.

Paul tells the Romans he is "not ashamed of the gospel of Christ, for it is the power of God to salvation for everyone who believes" (Rom. 1:16). In the next verse, he says, "For in it the righteousness of God is revealed from faith to faith" (Rom. 1:17), indicating that the salvation of verse 16 includes the gospel by which we are justified. Later in the book, Paul says, if "you believe in your heart that God has raised Him from the dead, you will be saved" (Rom. 10:9) and goes on to say, "For with the heart one believes unto righteousness" (Rom. 10:10). Paul is saying that when people *believe in the resurrection of Christ*, they are justified (see "unto righteousness").

Moreover, there is only one person in the New Testament called an evangelist, a man named Phillip (Acts 21:8). There is only one detailed incident of Philip leading someone to Christ (Acts 8:26-39). In that case, Philip preached about Jesus to an

Ethiopian eunuch (Acts 8:35), explaining to him Isaiah 53, the Old Testament prophecy of the Messiah's death.

More specifically, the passage was Isaiah 53:7-8. Luke records, "The place in the Scripture which he read was this: 'He was led as a sheep to the slaughter; and as a lamb before its shearer *is* silent, so He opened not His mouth. In His humiliation, His justice was taken away, and who will declare His generation? For His life is taken from the earth'" (Acts 8:33). In other words, Philip explained to the Ethiopian it was *Jesus* who was led as a sheep to the slaughter. Marshall says this passage "refers to a Servant of God who suffers humiliation of all kinds and bears the consequences of the sins of others; he thus makes some kind of atonement for their sins and is finally exalted by God." He adds that the particular verses cited are obscure; they describe the Servant remaining silent.

Can there be any doubt that Philip preached the death of Jesus to the Ethiopian eunuch? Is it not significant that the only case of someone called an evangelist in the New Testament, in the only detailed record of him leading someone to Christ, preached Jesus and His death?

The conclusion is clear. What Jesus commanded, and what the apostles and others did, was to preach the gospel, defined as Jesus died for our sins and rose from the dead, and what people did was to *believe* in Jesus, who died for their sins and rose from the dead to be saved.

The issue is not what the minimum people have to believe is to be saved. The issue is what we are commanded to preach. The issue is not what people understood *before* Christ was crucified. The issue is what we are commanded to preach *after* Christ was crucified. From the passages on the Great Commission, the preaching of Peter, the practice of Paul, and the proclamation of Philip, it is plain that we are to preach the death and resurrection of Christ. In the Gospel of John, before Jesus began His ministry, John the Baptist preached, "Behold! The Lamb of God who takes away the sin of the world!" (Jn. 1:29). Certainly, we should point people to the Lamb, who was slain and rose from the dead. Some wish to debate, "What is the minimum people have to believe to be saved?" Should we not be asking, "What is the *norm—for today?*"

From a New Testament point of view, not only should the death and resurrection of Christ be proclaimed in evangelism, but believers are to be constantly reminded of the death and resurrection of Christ. Immediately after conversion, believers are to be baptized. Baptism is a picture of a believer's death and resurrection with Christ (Rom. 6:1-11). Then, believers are to assemble *every week* to partake of the Lord's Supper. The very *purpose* of the weekly gathering is to observe the Lord's Table (Acts 20:7)! The Lord's Table is a memorial to constantly remind believers that Jesus died for their sins (Mt. 26:28; Mk. 14:24; Lk. 22:20; 1 Cor. 11:24-26). In fact, Paul says, "For as often as you eat this bread and drink this cup, you proclaim the Lord's death till He comes" (1 Cor. 11:26). After that, believers are to be taught that the death of Christ is the basis for not only salvation (Rom. 3:24-26), but sanctification (Rom. 6:1-11), suffering (1 Pet. 3:17-

41), etc. Believers are to get to know Christ, the power of His resurrection, and the fellowship of His suffering (Phil. 3:10).

No wonder Paul says, "For I determined not to know anything among you except Jesus Christ and Him crucified" (1 Cor. 2:2). The cross is critical. The cross is central. We dare not leave it out of baptism, the Lord's Table, the teaching ministry on the spiritual life—and evangelism. Proclaim it from the housetops. Jesus died for the sins of the world and rose from the dead.

CHAPTER 5

THE DEFINITION OF BELIEVE

The discussion concerning what to believe could leave the impression that the definition of "believe" is simply believing facts. Is that all there is to saving faith? What exactly is the definition of the Greek word translated "believe?" What does John mean by "believe?" To complicate matters, there are several different constructions of "believe" in the Gospel of John. What is the significance of the various constructions?

The Greek Word

The Greek Word In all one hundred occurrences of "believe" in John's Gospel, the same Greek verb is used. John never uses the Greek noun faith. There is no difference in the meaning between the verb and the noun. As Bromiley observes, "Paul regularly has the noun whereas John prefers the verb, though with no essential difference of meaning" (Bromiley, vol. II, p. 270). At any rate, John only uses the verb in his Gospel.

The Meaning The Greek word translated "believe" has four basic meanings: 1) "believe (in) something, be convinced of something. 2) "believe (in), trust." When used in the religious sense, it is "belief in a special sense, as faith in the Divinity that lays special emphasis on trust in his power and nearness to help, in addition to being convinced that he exists and that his revelations or disclosures are true." 3) "Entrust something to someone." 4) A unique use that means something like "one trusts himself to eat" something (Arndt and Gingrich, 2nd ed., pp. 660-662).

In a later edition by Danker, the second entry has been changed to read, "to entrust oneself to an entity in complete confidence, believe (in), trust, w. implication of total commitment to the one who is trusted. In our lit. God and Christ are objects of this type of faith that relies on their power and nearness to help, in addition to being convinced that their revelations or disclosures are true" (Arndt and Gingrich, 3rd ed., p. 817), but that change has been criticized as being theologically motivated (Makidon, vol. 17, pp. 17-18). The statement about "with implication of total commitment" is only an "implication" if a theological presupposition is brought to the definition. Even the statement itself calls it an "implication." It is not part of the definition. Nevertheless, both editions agree one of the meanings of "believe" is "trust."

The Moulton and Milligan Greek lexicon does not hesitate to translate the Greek word for "believe" as "trust" (Moulton and Milligan, p. 514). The Liddell and Scott Greek-English lexicon says "believe" means "to trust, trust to," or "in," "put faith in, rely on, believe" a person or thing (Liddell and Scott, p. 641).

A statement in Kittel says, "From a purely formal standpoint, there is nothing very distinctive" in the usage of the New Testament writings compared to secular Greek usage. As in secular Greek, it means 'to rely on,' 'to trust,' and 'to believe'" (Kittel, vol. 6, p.

203).

No dictionary defines a word as a given author uses it or as it appears in a given sentence. Dictionaries only list possible meanings, called the "field of meaning." The interpreter of a text must determine which meaning an author is using. For example, the word "trunk" can mean a tree's main stem, a human being's torso, a large box used as luggage or for storage, a compartment of an automobile, or the long, flexible snout of an elephant. Oh yes, and men wear swimming trunks! The interpreter must decide which of these meanings is the meaning in a particular sentence. The dictionary does not determine meaning; usage determines meaning.

The Different Constructions

The several different constructions of "believe" in the Greek text of the Gospel of John are apparent in the English translation. The word "believe" is used absolutely; what is believed is not stated, but, in some cases, the content of belief is evident from the context. Believe is sometimes followed by "that" and sometimes by "in." In the one hundred appearances of "believe" listed in the previous chapter, these differences are noted [cf. "believe that" (oti) and "believe in" (eis)]. The question is, "What is the significance of these differences?

Believe That The construction "believe that" occurs twelve times in John's Gospel.

1. "Therefore, I said to you that you will die in your sins;

for if you do not believe <u>that I am *He*</u>, you will die in your sins" (8:24).

2. "But if I do, though you do not believe Me, believe the works, that you may know and believe <u>that the Father *is* in Me, and I in Him</u>" (10:38)

3. "She said to Him, 'Yes, Lord, I believe <u>that You are the Christ, the Son of God, who is to come into the world</u>'" (11:27).

4. "And I know that You always hear Me, but because of the people who are standing by I said *this*, that they may believe <u>that You sent Me</u>" (11:42).

5. "Now I tell you before it comes, that when it does come to pass, you may believe <u>that I am *He*</u>" (13:19)

6. "Do you not believe <u>that I am in the Father, and the Father in Me</u>? The words that I speak to you I do not speak on My own *authority;* but the Father who dwells in Me does the works" (14:10).

7. Believe Me <u>that I *am* in the Father and the Father in Me</u>, or else believe Me for the sake of the works themselves" (14:11)

8. "Or the Father Himself loves you, because you have loved Me, and have believed <u>that I came forth from God</u>" (16:27).

9. "Now we are sure that You know all things, and have no need that anyone should question You. By this we believe <u>that You came forth from God</u>" (16:30).

10. "For I have given to them the words which You have given Me; and they have received *them,* and have known surely that I came forth from You; and they have believed <u>that You sent Me</u>" (17:8).

11. "that they all may be one, as You, Father, *are* in Me, and I in You; that they also may be one in Us, that the world may believe <u>that You sent Me</u>" (17:21).

12. "But these are written that you may believe <u>that Jesus is the Christ, the Son of God</u>, and that believing you may have life in His name." (20:31)

John 5:24 contains "believe that," but it is a different Greek construction.

The "believe that" construction delineates facts to be believed. These facts are that Jesus is the Christ, the Son of God (11:27; 20:31), who is God (8:24; 10:38; 13:19; 14:10, 14:11) sent by the Father (11:42; 16:27, 16:30; 17:8, 17:21).

Believe in The construction "believe in" occurs thirty-seven times in the Gospel of John.

believed in (eis) Him (2:11).

believes in (eis) Him (3:15)

believes in (eis) Him (3:16).

believes in (eis) the Son (3:36)

believed in (eis) Him (4:39)

believe in (eis) Him (6:29)

believes in (eis) Me (6:35)

believes in (eis) Him (6:40)

believes in (eis) Me (6:47)

did not believe in (eis) Him (7:5)

believed in (eis) Him (7:26)

believes in (eis) Me (7:38)

believing in (eis) Him (7:39)

believed in (eis) Him (7:48)
believe in (eis) Him (8:30)
believe in (eis) the Son of God (9:35).
believe in (eis) Him (9:36)
believe in (eis) Him (10:42)
believes in (eis) Me (11:25)
believes in (eis) Me (11:26)
believed in (eis) Him (11:45)
believe in (eis) Him (11:48)
believed in (eis) Jesus (12:11)
believe in the (eis) light
not believe in (eis) Him" (12:37)
believed in (eis) Him" (12:42)
believes in (eis) Me (12:44)
believes not in (eis) Me (12:44)
believes in (eis) Me (12:46)
believe in (eis) Me (14:1)
believes in (eis) Me (14:12)
do not believe in (eis) Me (16:9)
believe in (eis) Me (17:20)

There are places in the Gospel of John where "believe in" (eis) and the simple "believe" without being followed by either "in" or "that" are used interchangeably, John 3:18 says, "He who *believes in* (eis) Him is not condemned, "but he who does not *believe* is condemned already, because he has not *believed in* (eis) the name of the only begotten Son of God." In this statement, there is no question but that "believe in" (eis) and the simple "believe" are used of the believing that gains eternal life. In this case, since "believe in" (eis) appears first, is not the simple "believe" a synonym for "believe in" (eis), especially because in the same breath, John returns to "believe in" (eis)? John 8:30-31 has also been used to support the notion that there is no difference between "believe in" and "believe." Those verses say, "Many believed in (eis) Him" (8:30) and "Jesus said to those Jews who believed Him." Since "believe in" (eis) is used first, is not "believe Him" shorthand for believing in Him?

At face value, it certainly appears that John is emphasizing "believing in" Jesus. What is the implication of this construction? Scholars differ concerning the significance between "believe that" and "believe in." For a summary, see Morris' "Additional Note E: Believing" (Morris, pp. 335-337).

Some scholars say there is no difference between "believe that" and "believe in." Bultmann claims that "to believe the words of Jesus" is materially the same as "to believe in Jesus." According to him, "The linguistic variation contains no material distinction." He says, "To believe Jesus when He preaches (or tells the truth, 8:40, 45), or to believe His Word (2:22) or words" (5:47), is equivalent to "believing in the Jesus who is proclaimed." He supports this conclusion in a footnote by pointing to John 8:30-31. [G. Kittel, G. W. Bromiley & G. Friedrich, Ed. *Theological Dictionary of the New Testament* (electronic ed.) Grand Rapids, MI: Eerdmans, vol. 6, p. 222.].

Clark, a philosophy professor, argues that "believe that" and "believe in" are used interchangeably (Clark, 1983, p. 101; 1990, p. 146). There are no different kinds of faith. Faith is faith. Faith is "assent to an understood proposition" (Clark, 1983, p. 118). A person can be identified only by a set of propositions (Clark, 1983, p. 50). The difference is the object of belief. The Pharisees believed Jesus died; they did not believe He died for our sins (Clark, 1983, p. 104).

Others disagree. The Arndt and Gingrich say with the preposition (eis), "believe" means "dependent on," "put one's trust in" (Arndt and Gingrich 2nd, p. 660). According to the Abbott-Smith Greek lexicon, the Greek word translated "believe" means "to have faith (in), to believe" and, with a preposition attached, it means "to believe in" or "to believe on," "expressing personal trust and reliance as distinct from mere credence or belief" (Abbott-Smith, pp. 361-362).

Moulton suggests that "believe in" reflects the Hebrew and Aramaic phrase "trust in" and signifies "personal trust" (J. H. Moulton, *A Grammar of the New Testament Greek*, Vol. I. p. 68, cited by Morris, p. 336, fn. 132). Dodd says that "believe" connotes simple credence, but "believe in" is "personal trust or reliance" inherent in the Hebrew and Aramaic phrase "trust in" (C. H. Dodd, *The Interpretation of the New Testament*, p. 183, cited by Morris, p. 335, fn. 131). Bromiley says when the verb "believe" is followed by a preposition such as "on" (eis in Jn. 3:16, epi in Acts 16:31) or "in" (en in Mark 1:5), it expresses reliance or trust (Bromiley in *ISBE*, vol. II, p. 270. See also Berkhof, pp. 494-95, Erickson, p. 940).

Which view is correct? To answer that question, several things need to be noted. For one thing, "believe in" is a unique construction. Dodd does not find "believe in" (eis) in either secular Greek or the Greek translation of the Old Testament, the LXX. (Dodd, p. 183, cited by Morris, p. 335, fn. 131). Moreover, John uses this unique construction 37 out of 100 times. Does not the fact that John uses a unique construction so many times imply there is a difference between "believe that" and "believe in"?

Also, is it not significant that Greek lexicons conclude such things as: when used in the religious sense, "believe (in)," has a "special emphasis on trust" (Arndt and Gingrich 2nd, p. 661) and "believe in" means, "personal trust and reliance as distinct from mere credence or belief" (Abbott-Smith, pp. 361-362).

In addition, it should be noted that the Gospel of John uses synonyms for "believe." Figures for faith include asking (4:10), drinking water (4:13-14), doing the good thing (5:29), and work (6:20-29). Jesus tells people to labor for eternal life (6:27), but clarifies that the Son of Man *gives* eternal life, indicating it is a gift (6:27). He says, "I am the bread of life. He who comes to Me shall never hunger, and he who believes in Me shall never thirst" (6:35). Coming to Christ and believing in Him are synonymous in this statement, as are "never hungering and never thirsting" (6:53). He says, "This is the bread which comes down from heaven, that one may eat of it and not die. I am the living bread that came down from heaven. If anyone eats of this bread, he will live forever; and the bread that I shall give is My flesh, which I shall give for the life of the world" (6:50-51). He says, "Whoever eats My flesh and drinks My blood has eternal life, and I will raise him up at the last day" (6:54). Jesus uses the figure of walking as a synonym for faith (12:35), which is clear from the next verse (12:36; cf. also 5:11). He even uses "following" as a synonym for believing (10:27). Asking, drinking, doing, working, laboring, coming, eating, walking and following are figures of speech for believing, indicating that believing is more than believing a proportion. These metaphors convey the concept of appropriation by trusting or depending on something or someone. For example, eating bread indicates dependence on bread for life. On the other hand, these metaphors should not be taken to teach that anyone can do anything meritorious; eternal life is not by works. It is a gift (4:10).

There may be some truth to Clark's contention that a person can be identified only by a set of propositions, but John seems to be making the point that while belief involves accepting certain propositions about Jesus, what he is emphasizing is that to obtain eternal life, one must *believe in* Jesus, that is, trust Jesus for it. Granted, John writes to get people to "believe that" Jesus is the Christ, the Son of God (30:21), but how could he be any more clear or emphatic that eternal life is gained by trusting a person, not just believing a proposition about that person than he does by saying over and over again that what he is talking about is *believing in Jesus.* Perhaps a philosopher can argue that, philosophically, faith is faith, and that a person can be identified only by a set of propositions, but John prefers to speak of believing *in* a person.

Therefore, faith involves *both* "believing that" and "believing in" (Bruce, p. 12). The difference is that "believe that" conveys the idea of being convinced that something is true, while "believe in" conveys the concepts of trust, reliance, or dependence. As Erickson says, "The type of faith necessary for salvation involves believing that and believing in or assenting to facts and trusting in a person" (Erickson, p. 940).

On a practical level, it is plain that there is a difference between believing facts and trusting those facts. I can believe the plane will get me there, but I do not trust it to do it. John desires his readers believe that Jesus is the Christ, the Son of God, who died for the sins of the world and rose from the dead and he wants them to *trust Jesus for eternal life.*

The Traditional Explanation

Traditionally, theologians have said that before people can believe something or trust someone, they must know something. Therefore, there are three elements of faith. The famous theologian Charles Hodge says faith includes knowledge (perception of the truth), assent (persuasion of the truth of the object of faith), and trust (reliance)" (Hodge on Romans, p. 29). Some want to stop at the second element, making faith mere mental assent. Others want to make the third element "commitment," which is arrived at by coming to this discussion with the theological presupposition that unless there is continuance, there is not "real" faith. The New Testament does not support such a theological presupposition. Faith consists of knowledge, assent, and trust.

Believing assumes knowledge. In the Gospel of John, hearing sometimes precedes believing (5:24, see Rom. 10:14), and so does seeing (6:40). So, while the word "believe" does not include knowledge, at the same time, it is self-evident that believing assumes knowledge. People can't believe something they do not know! In the Gospel of John, the knowledge necessary to obtain eternal life is that Jesus is the Christ, the Son of God. He is presented as the God/man who died for sin and rose from the dead.

Believing is accepting something as true. It is "believing that." People cannot "believe" without "belief!" Pointing out that modern preachers say faith is not assent to a creed but confidence in a person, J. Gresham Machen says, "It is impossible to have confidence in a person without assenting to a creed." He says that faith is more than accepting a creed, but he insists that it always involves accepting one. In his words, "Assent to certain propositions is not the whole of faith, but it is an absolutely necessary element in faith" (Machen, pp. 47-48), and "faith is always based upon knowledge" (Machen, p. 88).

The believing involved in obtaining eternal life includes trust. It is trusting Jesus Christ *for* life. One of the clearest statements of this in the New Testament is Paul's statement that he is a pattern "to those who are going to believe on (epi) Him *for* (eis) everlasting life" (1 Tim. 1:16 NKJV). The Greek preposition Paul uses for "believe on" (epi) means "on, upon" and the preposition eis is used for intent or purpose (Strong).

Hence, traditionally, theologians have said faith involves knowledge, mental assent, and *trust*. The Westminster Shorter Catechism says, "Faith in Jesus Christ is the saving grace, whereby we receive and rest upon Him alone for salvation, as He is offered to us in the gospel." Berkhof defines saving faith "as a certain conviction wrought in the heart by the Holy Spirit, as to the truth of the gospel, and a hearty reliance (trust) on the promises of God in Christ" (Berkhof, p. 502). Grudem uses knowledge, approval, and personal trust. He contends that the first two are insufficient for eternal life and only when the first two are combined with the third (personal, volitional trust) can a person be granted eternal life (Grudem, pp. 709-12).

Ryrie says, "*Trust* may be particularly appropriate today, for the words *believe* and *faith* sometimes seem to be watered down so that they convey little more than knowing facts" (Ryrie, *So Great Salvation*, p. 121). Ryrie also says, "To have faith in Christ unto salvation means to have confidence that He can remove the guilt of sin and grant eternal life" (Ryrie in *Basic Theology*, p. 326. See an almost identical statement in *So Great Salvation*, p. 119). In his book entitled *So Great Salvation*, he states, "When a person gives credence to the historical facts that Christ died and rose from the dead and the doctrinal fact that this was for his sins, he is trusting his eternal destiny to the reliability of those truths" (Ryrie, *So Great Salvation*, p 30). Later in the book, Ryrie says, "The issue is whether or not you believe that His death paid for your sin and by believing in Him you can have forgiveness and eternal life (Ryrie, *So Great Salvation*, p. 119).

Hodges says that faith is "the inward conviction of what God says to us in the gospel is true" (Hodges, *Absolutely Free*, p. 31) and "Saving faith is taking God at His Word in the gospel" (Hodges, *Absolutely Free*, p. 33). In discussing Martha's confession of faith in John 11, Hodges says, "Thus, by believing the amazing facts about the person of Christ, Martha was *trusting* Him. She was placing her eternal destiny in His hands" (Hodges, *Absolutely Free*, p. 39).

Summary: Believing is more than believing facts; it involves having information ("hearing" and "seeing"), being persuaded that it is true, and trusting something or someone.

The believing that brings eternal life is believing that Jesus is the Son of God, who died and rose from the dead, and trusting Him for the gift of eternal life. It is placing one's eternal destiny in the hands of the Son of God, who died for your sins and rose from the dead. It is about believing in the facts about Jesus Christ and trusting in Jesus Christ. It is not just believing a proposition; it is trusting a person.

CHAPTER 6

CONCLUSION

Taken as a whole, the Gospel of John presents Jesus as the Christ, the Son of God (which means He is God the Son), who died for the sin of the world and rose from the dead, and that all who *trust* Him *for* eternal life have it (3:36). Based on the Gospel of John, as well as other passages, there are two practical conclusions.

First, we should *present* the good news that Jesus, the Christ, the Son of God, became a man, died for the sins of the world, and rose from the dead. Taken as a complete book, as it was intended to be, it is clear that John wants his readers to *know* who Jesus is and what He did in dying and being raised from the dead. God wants people to "*hear* the word of the gospel and believe" (Acts 15:7, italics added). Wiersbe says, "The substitutionary death of Jesus Christ is a key doctrine in John's Gospel. Jesus would die for the world (3:16; 6:51), for His sheep (10:11, 15), for the nation (11:50-52), and for His friends (15:12)" (Wiersbe, p. 79).

Second, we should *proclaim* salvation by faith alone. What must people know and believe? Obviously, they must know about Jesus (14:6; Acts 4:12). Furthermore, John clearly says he wrote so that people might believe that Jesus is the Christ, the Son of God (20:31). Does not John present Jesus as the Christ *who died for the sins of the world?* Jesus says, "It was *necessary* for the Christ to suffer and to rise from the dead" (Lk. 24:46, italics added). According to Jesus and John, Christ is the One who died for sin and rose from the dead.

Paul says the Corinthians were saved by *believing the gospel* (1 Cor. 15:1-2), which he defines as "Christ died for our sins according to the Scriptures" (1 Cor. 15:3) and "He rose again the third day according to the Scriptures" (1 Cor. 15:4). Paul specifically says that when people believe that God raised Jesus from the dead (Rom. 10:9), they are declared righteous (Rom. 10:10).

Part of proclaiming salvation by faith alone in Christ alone is to clearly communicate the concept of *trusting* Jesus Christ *for* eternal life (1 Tim. 1:16). This is an important point. It is not enough to believe that Jesus died for the sin and rose from the dead. The faith that saves is the faith that *trusts Jesus Christ,* who died to pay for sin and rose from the dead *to save me.* Many believe that Jesus died and rose, but they are trusting something *they do* to get them to heaven. That will not do. One way to clearly communicate that message is to emphasize that salvation is not by works. It is a gift (4:10; Rom. 6:23; Eph. 2:8-9).

By the way, the expression "eternal life" can be confusing. A fellow once said to me, "I thought everyone lived forever." In the Gospel of John, the issue is eternal life; in the book of Acts, the message is about the forgiveness of sins (Acts 2:38; 3:19; 5:31; 10:43; 13:38). In the book of Romans, the issue is justification. To keep it as simple as possible, I tell people they must *trust* Christ, who died for their sins and rose from the dead, *to get to heaven* (Jn. 14:1-6).

Bromiley says, "To have faith in a person is to believe certain things about this person, his nature, word, and work. It is more than this, but it is certainly no less. One does not need to know everything, nor even everything that is knowable, but it is essential to know and believe something. One cannot really trust in Jesus Christ without believing that he is the Messiah, the incarnate Son, the crucified and risen Savior" (Bromiley, *ISBE*, vol. II, p. 271).

BIBLIOGRAPHY

Abbott-Smith, G. *A Manual Greek Lexicon of the New Testament.* Edinburgh: T & T. Clark, 1960.

Alford, Henry. *The Greek New Testament*, Vol. I. Chicago: Moody Press, 1968.

William F. Arndt and F. Wilbur Gingrich, trans. by Walter Bauer, *A Greek-English Lexicon of the New Testament and other Early Christian Literature*, 2nd ed.

Beasley-Murray, John. *Word Biblical Commentary.* Waco, TX: Word Books, Publishers.

Berkhof, L., *Systematic Theology.* Grand Rapids: Wm. B. Eerdmans Publishing, 1961.

Bromiley, G. W., "Faith," *International Standard Bible Encyclopedia*, vol. II, Grand Rapids: William B. Eerdmans Publishing Company, 1982.

Bruce, F. F. *The Gospel of John*, Grand Rapids: William B. Eerdmans Publishing Company, 1983.

Clark, Gordon. *Faith and Saving Faith*, Jefferson, Maryland, The Trinity Foundation, 1983,

__________. *What is Saving Faith?* Jefferson, Maryland, The Trinity Foundation, 1990,

Clark, John C. "Martin Luther's View of Cross-Bearing." *Bibliotheca Sacra*, 163:651, July-September 2006.

Cocoris, G. Michael. *Evangelism: A Biblical Approach.* Chicago: Moody Press, 1984.

Dana, H. E. and Mantey, Julius R. *A Manual Grammar of the Greek New Testament*. New York: The Macmillan Company, 1959.

Erickson, Millard J. *Christian Theology*. Grand Rapids: Baker Book House, 1990.

France, R. T. *The Gospel According to Matthew*, Grand Rapids: William B. Eerdmans Publishing Company, 1985, 1999 reprint.

Godet, F. L. *Commentary on the Gospel of John*. 2 vol. Grand Rapids: Zondervan Publishing House. 1883.

Grudem, Wayne. *Systematic Theology*. Grand Rapids, MI: Zondervan, 2000.

Hodges, Zane C. *Absolutely Free*. Grand Rapids: Zondervan Publishing House, 1989.

___________. *The Hungry Inherit*, Chicago: Moody Press, 1972.

Kittel, G., W. Bromiley & G. Friedrich, Ed. *Theological Dictionary of the New Testament* (electronic ed.) Grand Rapids, MI: Eerdmans, vol. 6.

Liddell H. G., and Scott. *An Intermediate Greek-English Lexicon*, New York: Harper & Brothers, 1894.

Machen, J. Gresham. *What is Faith?* Grand Rapids: William B. Eerdmans Publishing Company, 1925.

Makidon, Michael. "Soteriological Concerns with Bauer's Greek Lexicon," *Journal of the Grace Evangelical Society*, Autumn 2004, vol. 17, pp. 17-18.

Martinez, G. Ted. "The Purpose of John's Gospel: Part One," *Michigan Theological Journal*, Vol. 3:1, Spring 1992.

______________. "The Purpose of John's Gospel: Part Two," *Michigan Theological Journal*, Vol. 3:2, Fall 1992.

Moulton, James Hope and Milligan, George. *The Vocabulary of the Greek Testament*. Grand Rapids: William Eerdmans Publishing Company, 1972.

Merrill C. Tenney. *John: The Gospel of Belief,* Grand Rapids: William Eerdmans Publishing Company, 1960.

Morris, Leon. *The Gospel According to John*, Grand Rapids: William Eerdmans Publishing Company, 1984.

Plummer, A. *The Gospel According to St. John*, Cambridge: University, 1902.

Ryrie, Charles C. *Basic Theology*, Wheaton, Illinois: Victor Books, 1986.

______________. *So Great Salvation*. Wheaton, Illinois: Victor Books, 1989.

Stephen Smalley. "Keeping Up with Recent Studies—XII. St. John's Gospel," *The Expository Times*, 97, 1986, pp. 102-108.

Tasker, R. V. G, *The Gospel According to St. John* in the Tyndale New Testament Commentaries series, Grand Rapids: William Eerdmans Publishing Company, 1986.

Traina, Robert A. *Methodical Bible Study*, New York: Biblical Seminary, 1957.

Westcott, B. F. *The Gospel According to John*. London: James Clarke, 1958.

Wiersbe, Warren W. *Be Alive*. David C. Cook, Colorado Springs, CO, 1986.

About The Author

G. Michael Cocoris is a gifted communicator. He can make even complicated subjects simple, clear, and practical. His breadth of experience has allowed him to relate to a wide range of audiences.

Michael received a Bachelor of Arts degree from Tennessee Temple University, a Master of Theology degree from Dallas Seminary, and a Doctorate of Divinity from Biola University. He traveled the United States for over a dozen years as a speaker. He has also been a seminary professor, visiting lecturer, and world traveler, including hosting tours to Israel and China.

Michael has pastored three churches, including a rural church when he was in seminary, an urban church, the historic Church of the Open Door, first in downtown Los Angeles and later in Glendora, California, and a suburban church, the Lindley Church in Tarzana California, a suburb of Los Angeles. While at the Church of Open Door, he had a daily radio broadcast.

Michael has written numerous magazine articles, mainly for *Biblical Research Monthly*. He has authored a number of books, including *Seventy Years on Hope Street, A History of the Church of the Open Door; How To Live A Biblical Spiritual Life, Clarifying the Confusion; Repentance, The Most Misunderstood Word in the Bible; Evangelism: A Biblical Approach; The Salvation Controversy; Lordship Salvation: Is It Biblical?; The Books of the Bible, the Subject, Structure, Situation, and Significant Verses of Each Book; Psalms, A Song for Every Situation, Each Summarized on One Page; and Counseling Theories, A Biblical Evaluation.* In addition, he was a contributor to The *NKJV Study Bible* and *Nelson's New Illustrated Bible Commentary*.

Michael is the pastor of the Lindley Church in Tarzana, California. He and his wife, Patricia, live in Santa Monica, California.

www.ingramcontent.com/pod-product-compliance
Lightning Source LLC
Chambersburg PA
CBHW050011070726
47598CB00014B/667